WYOMING TRIVIA

BRIAN DAY

RIVERBEND
PUBLISHING

Dedication

This book is dedicated to my beautiful wife Joelle, who provided the computer on which this book was created as well as a steady flow of reference material to her husband sequestered in a dark corner of the house on many a winter's night.

This book is also dedicated to my parents Keith and Ethel, who always encouraged their children to explore the world and reflect it in whatever creative means that suited them best.

Contents

GEOGRAPHY

Q. Wyoming is a Native American word roughly translated as "a wide prairie place." From what tribal language did it originate?
A. It is an Algonquin or Delaware Indian word.

Q. Where were the Algonquin and Delaware tribes located?
A. They were located in the areas of present-day New York and Pennsylvania.

Q. How did Wyoming get its name?
A. A county in Pennsylvania—and a particularly wide valley in that county—were known to local Indians as "Wyoming." When modern-day Wyoming was designated a territory, Congressman James M. Ashley of Ohio said that because much of the new territory was similar to the Wyoming Valley in Pennsylvania, the territory should bear the same name. After much debate, Senator James W. Nye from Nevada finally confirmed "Wyoming" as the territory name in 1868.

Q. What other names were proposed for the future Wyoming Territory in the late 1860s?
A. Wyoming was almost named "Lincoln," "Cheyenne," and "Shoshone."

Q. When did Wyoming become a state?
A. Wyoming became a state on July 10, 1890.

Q. From what addition to the United States—the Louisiana Purchase, the Oregon Acquisition, the Texas Annexation, or the Mexican Cession—did the land that comprises Wyoming come from?
A. Wyoming is the only state to contain land from all four additions to the United States.

Q. How many states had joined the Union before it?
A. Wyoming was the 44th state to enter the Union.

Q. What state preceded Wyoming in entering the Union?
A. Idaho entered the Union just seven days before Wyoming, on July 3, 1890.

Q. What is Wyoming's official nickname?
A. Wyoming is known as the Equality State because it was the first state to allow women to vote.

Q. What was a major cause for resistance to allowing Wyoming to become a state?
A. Wyoming had allowed women's suffrage, or the right to vote, since 1869. The rest of the United States did not want to accept this condition.

Q. What was the response of the Wyoming territorial government to the other states' resentment over women's suffrage?
A. The territorial government said, "We will remain out of the Union a hundred years, rather than come in without the women."

Q. Who was elected justice of the peace in South Pass City, Wyoming, in 1870?
A. Esther Hobart Morris became the first woman to serve in a public office anywhere in the United States.

Q. What did Esther Hobart Morris wear, with her calico dress and shawl, to her first day as justice of the peace?
A. She wore a green necktie.

Q. What "first" for women occurred in 1870 in Laramie, Wyoming?
A. The first women served on a court jury anywhere in the United States.

Q. What "first" for women occurred in 1871 in Laramie?
A. Louiza Swain became the first woman to vote in a general election in the United States.

Q. Where was the first woman elected as a city mayor in the United States?
A. Susan Whissler was elected in Dayton, Wyoming.

Q. When was Susan Whissler elected?
A. She was elected in 1911.

Q. What was unique about the city government of Jackson Hole, Wyoming, in 1920?
A. All of its officials and personnel were women.

Q. Who was the first woman to become governor of a state?
A. Nellie Taylor Ross became the first female governor of a state when she was elected governor of Wyoming in 1925.

Q. Wyoming's prominent symbol is the Bucking Horse and Rider, seen on its license plates as well as other locations. Where was this symbol first in recorded use?
A. The Bucking Horse and Rider were first drawn by First Sergeant George N. Ostrom for use as an insignia for the Wyoming National Guard in France and Germany during World War I. The insignia was officially adopted by the United States Army and has represented Wyoming troops in all actions ever since.

Q. Does the horse in the insignia have a name?
A. Most people believe it represents a bucking horse from the early 1900s that could not be ridden. The horse was named Steamboat.

Q. When did the Bucking Horse and Rider first make its appearance on Wyoming's license plates?
A. The Bucking Horse and Rider symbol first appeared on Wyoming license plates in 1936. Wyoming license plates were the first state plates to utilize a symbolic image of the state. Other states soon followed suit. The Wyoming license horse and rider was actually created from a photograph of Albert "Stub" Farlow aboard a bronc named Deadman.

Q. How is Wyoming's use of this symbol protected?
A. The Bucking Horse and Rider have been copyrighted for Wyoming since 1936.

Q. What threatened Wyoming's right to the symbol in 1994?
A. A company in Beverly Hills, California, tried to register the Bucking Horse and Rider trademark. Its efforts were defeated and Wyoming's rights to the insignia were further legally protected.

Q. Wyoming prison inmates manufacture the license plates for Wyoming automobiles. What other objects do they manufacture which are common sights on Wyoming roadways?
A. The prisoners manufacture the many "point of interest" historic signs seen throughout Wyoming.

Q. How many four-year universities are located in Wyoming?
A. Only one, the University of Wyoming, is located in Laramie.

Q. How many two-year colleges are located in Wyoming?
A. Seven junior college campuses exist in the state, at Casper, Cheyenne, Powell, Riverton, Rock Springs, Sheridan, and Torrington. Three sub-campuses exist at Gillette, Pine Bluffs, and Laramie.

Q. Where was the first American Legion Post established in the United States?
A. The first American Legion Post in the United States was Ferdinand Branstetter Post Number One of Van Tassell, Wyoming.

Q. When was this American Legion post established?
A. 1919.

Q. Why is it named after Ferdinand Branstetter?
A. Ferdinand Branstetter, a native of Van Tassell, Wyoming, was the first soldier to die in the trenches of World War I.

Q. According to Wyoming state law, how many people must live in a settlement for it to be classified as a city?
A. An official Wyoming city must be larger than 4,000 people.

Q. How many people must be living in a settlement to classify it as a town?
A. A Wyoming town must have 150 or more people. Any settlement smaller than 150 people is considered a village.

Q. Where is the smallest town in the United States with a post office?
A. Lost Springs, Wyoming, is the smallest incorporated town in the U.S. with a post office.

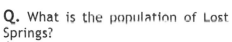

Q. What is the population of Lost Springs?
A. Lost Springs currently has an official population of 1. It is one of three towns in the U.S. with an official population of 1.

Q. What are the other two towns with only one resident in the U.S.?
A. Hibberts, Maine, and Erving's Landing, New Hampshire, are the other two U.S. towns with only one resident.

Q. Where does Wyoming rank in population among the fifty states?
A. Wyoming is ranked 50th. It is the least populated state, containing about 500,000 people.

Q. What is the density of people per square mile in Wyoming?
A. Wyoming contains 5.1 people per square mile.

Q. What is the population of Vermont, which has the second lowest population in the United States?
A. Vermont has 623,908 residents.

Q. What is the population density of Vermont?
A. Vermont has 65.8 people per square mile.

Q. What is the population density in New Jersey, the most densely populated state?
A. New Jersey contains 1,134.4 people per square mile.

Q. What is the population density in Alaska, which has the fourth lowest population of the fifty states?
A. The population density of Alaska is 1.1 people per square mile.

Q. How many people visited Yellowstone National Park in 2006?
A. 2,870,293 people visited Yellowstone Park—nearly six times the population of Wyoming.

Q. Where does the tourism industry rank in the percentage of state income generated in Wyoming?
A. Tourism ranks second in income-production in Wyoming.

Q. What is the leading industry in Wyoming?
A. Mining and energy production is the number-one income-producing industry in Wyoming. Mineral extraction generated $8,265,000,000 in 2005, the most recent year for which complete figures were available.

Q. Wyoming is known as the Cowboy State as well as the Equality State. Where do ranching and agriculture rank in income production in the state economy?
A. Agriculture ranks a distant third behind tourism.

Q. Are there more people of Native American descent or of Hispanic descent living in Wyoming?
A. As of 2004, 2.2 percent of Wyoming's population was of Native American descent, while 6.7 percent was of Hispanic descent.

Q. How many Native American reservations are located in Wyoming?
A. Just one, the Wind River Reservation near Riverton, Wyoming. It is home to about 2,000 Shoshone and 3,500 Arapaho Indians.

Q. What does the name "Arapaho" mean?
A. "Arapaho" is a Crow Indian word describing the tattoos that the Arapaho Indians applied to their chests.

Q. What is ironic about the name Arapaho for this tribe?
A. This tribe of Native Americans could not pronounce "Arapaho" because they did not have the R or H sound in their language. They did not use the word "Arapaho" until they began to speak English after contact with white men.

Q. How many Native American tribes once occupied parts of Wyoming?
A. At least 13 tribes: Arapaho, Arikara, Bannock, Blackfoot, Cheyenne, Crow, Gros Ventre, Kiowa, Nez Perce, Sheepeater, Sioux, Shoshone, and Ute Indians have all inhabited parts of Wyoming at various times.

Q. What building became the temporary White House of the United States in 1903?
A. President Theodore Roosevelt stayed in the Inter-Ocean Hotel in Cheyenne, Wyoming, for three days in 1903.

Q. What was unique about the Inter-Ocean Hotel at this time?
A. This was the first hotel in the world to have electric lights.

Q. What Wyoming city is designated the Sagebrush Capital of the World?
A. Newcastle is the Sagebrush Capital of the World.

Q. What is the largest ecosystem in the United States?
A. The sagebrush ecosystem encompasses large sections of eleven western states.

Q. How long do sagebrush plants live?
A. An individual sagebrush plant may live 200 years or more.

Q. What wood mentioned as the material for Noah's Ark in the Old Testament is sagebrush related to?
A. That is wormwood.

Q. Where is the largest coal mine in the United States?
A. The North Antelope Rochelle Mine, located near Wright, Wyoming.

Q. How many of the top-ten producing coal mines of the United States are located in Wyoming?
A. All of them.

Q. How many of the top-sixty producing coal mines of the United States are located in Wyoming?
A. Fifteen.

Q. Where is the second-largest coal mine in the United States?
A. The Black Thunder Mine, located near Wright, Wyoming.

Q. What is the land area of Wright, Wyoming?
A. Wright sparsely covers an area of 2.7 square miles.

Q. What is the population of Wright?
A. About 1,300 people.

Q. How close is the nearest town to Wright?
A. The nearest town to Wright is about 35 miles away. Almost no one lives in the vast space around the town except for a few ranchers. The population density in this area of Wyoming is less than one person per square mile.

Q. What natural disaster devastated Wright on August 12, 2005?
A. A tornado stuck the tiny community and nearly destroyed it. Two people were killed.

Q. When was the first coal mine in Wyoming?
A. The first coal mine was started in Carbon in 1867, which was nine years before Custer's Last Stand.

Q. Where does Wyoming rank in coal production among the states?
A. First, with 405 million tons per week in 2005, or 35 percent of the coal produced in the entire United States.

Q. What is the second-largest coal producing state in the Union?
A. West Virginia is the second-largest producer of coal with a production of about 13 percent of the total U. S. production—less than half that of Wyoming's.

Q. Where is the largest iron ore mine west of the Missouri River?
A. The Sunrise Iron Ore Mine is located six miles north of Guernsey, Wyoming. This area contains some of the purest iron ore in the United States.

Q. The Indians were aware of the iron ore in this area of Wyoming even before white men arrived. What did they use it for?
A. The Indians used the hematite for red paint.

Q. Where is the largest agate mine in the U.S. located?
A. The Adams-Hartville agate mine is located near Guernsey, Wyoming.

Q. What are agates?
A. Agates are a striped or banded variety of quartz gems. They are formed when volcanic water with a high concentration of silica fills bubbles or pockets in lava or magma. Silica is the main ingredient in quartz, and settles out in bands or layers as the water evaporates.

Q. What color are the agates from this mine?
A. The stones are white with black specks, giving them the common name of "zebra stone."

Q. What unique method do rock hounds use to locate agates from the Sweetwater Agate Beds of the Rattlesnake Mountains of Wyoming?
A. The mineral collectors use black (ultraviolet) lights at night to spot the gems, which glow softly in the UV light due to the trace amounts of uranium they contain.

Q. What was the reason for the town of Encampment to be settled?
A. A large copper mine began near there in 1897. The smelter was located in Encampment.

Q. What man-made object spanned the Continental Divide near Encampment for sixteen miles?
A. Miners built an elevated tramway to carry copper ore from the mines into Encampment. A section of it still exists at the Grand Encampment Museum.

Q. Where is the largest area of unfenced land in the lower 48 states?
A. The Red Desert in southwest Wyoming contains the largest area of unfenced land in the lower 48 states.

Q. Is the Red Desert as big as a state?
A. No, the Red Desert is about half as big as Rhode Island.

Q. The mountain range between Cheyenne and Laramie is called the Vedauwoo (pronounced *vee-dah-voo*). The name is an Indian word. What does it mean?
A. Vedauwoo means "earth born."

Q. What is the name of the mountain range that runs through most of Yellowstone National Park?
A. The mountain range is called the Absaroka Mountains.

Q. What does Absaroka mean?
A. Absaroka is a Native American word for crow, designating the Crow Indian tribe, which occupied the area.

Q. What national forest do you drive through if you are approaching the east entrance to Yellowstone National Park from Cody, Wyoming?
A. The Shoshone National Forest.

Q. President Benjamin Harrison created the first of what in Wyoming in 1891?
A. He created the first national forest, which was the Shoshone National Forest.

Q. How large is the Shoshone National Forest?
A. The forest encompasses 2.5 million acres, or nearly the size of Connecticut.

Q. What place became the world's first national park?
A. Yellowstone National Park.

Q. What president designated Yellowstone as a national park?
A. President Ulysses S. Grant created the park in 1872. This was nearly four years before General George Armstrong Custer and part of the 7th Cavalry were defeated by Sioux and Cheyenne warriors at the Battle of the Little Bighorn (Custer's Last Stand) in southeastern Montana.

Q. Where is the oldest ranger station in the United States?
A. The Wapiti Ranger Station, the oldest ranger station in the U.S., is located about forty miles north-west of Cody on the way to Yellowstone National Park.

Q. What other Wyoming site was also a national first?
A. Devils Tower was designated the first national monument in 1906.

Q. Which president created this designation?
A. President Theodore Roosevelt used the newly created Antiq uities Act to give Devils Tower this designation.

Q. How tall is Devils Tower?
A. Devils Tower is 867 feet tall. That is nearly three times the height of the Statue of Liberty.

Q. What caused Devils Tower to form?
A. An intrusion of molten rock or magma thrust its way up toward the surface of the earth. Cooling extremely slowly, the igneous magma crystallized into phonolite porphyry. Over millions of years, the ground around the igneous rock eroded away, leaving the tower of columns that we see today.

Q. How far beneath the earth's surface was the magma formation originally before it was exposed by erosion?
A. The magma plug was one and a half miles beneath the surface.

Q. What is unique about the phonolite columns of Devils Tower?
A. The columns are the longest known exposed phonolite porphyry columns in the world. They are more than six hundred feet long and as much as twenty feet wide in places.

Q. What did the Indians call Devils Tower?
A. Some Native Americans called the rock monolith "Mateo Tipila," meaning Bear Lodge. Their mythology tells of a group of young girls who were saved from an attacking grizzly bear by praying to a rock that they had climbed upon for sanctuary. The rock responded by growing into the sky while the grizzly bear clawed at its sides, leaving the vertical cracks now visible in the monument's sides. The girls rose into the sky and became the star constellation known as the Pleiades, or The Seven Sisters.

Q. What object might a visitor notice at Devils Tower that he or she might also notice at the Medicine Wheel on top of the Bighorn Mountains of Wyoming?
A. Native Americans consider Devils Tower, as well as the Medicine Wheel, to be a significant spiritual location and often leave prayer bundles and flags tied in the trees and among the rocks around Tower. Please leave them untouched.

Q. Why is the monument called Devils Tower today?
A. In 1875 Col. Richard I. Dodge mis-translated another Indian name for the tower—"the bad god's tower"—into "Devils Tower."

Q. When was the tower first officially noted?
A. Even though Devils Tower was most certainly known of and visited by early mountain men and explorers, it was not mentioned historically until a United States Geological Survey team, led by Col. Dodge, visited the area in 1875. There was a previous survey party; their map said "Bear's Lodge."

Q. When was Devils Tower first climbed?
A. Two ranchers from the local area, William Rogers and Willard Ripley, devised a way to secure a wooden ladder to the side of the tower by driving wooden stakes into a crack. They *officially* climbed the tower on the Fourth of July in 1893, during a celebration held at the base of the tower.

Q. What object miraculously appeared at the top of the tower for Mr. Rogers to use when he arrived there?

A. On his ascent William Rogers carried an American flag, and when he reached the summit, he ran the flag up a flagpole that was there, much to the enjoyment of the crowd below. (Apparently, the two ranchers had been to the top the previous day and left the flagpole, but the earlier ascent was never acknowledged.)

Q. What happened to the flag?
A. Later that day the wind tore it loose from the pole and it drifted down to the celebrants. It was cut into pieces and sold as souvenirs.

Q. Who was the first woman to climb Devils Tower?
A. William Rogers' wife climbed the tower two years later, on July 4, 1895.

Q. Does the ladder still exist?
A. Some 200 feet of the ladder still exists and is visible clinging to the rock face near the top of the tower. The ladder is listed on the National Register of historic properties.

Q. When was Devils Tower first climbed without the use of the wooden ladder?
A. On June 28, 1937, Fritz Wiessner, Lawrence Coveney, and William P. House of the American Alpine Club of New York City climbed the south side of Devils Tower in four hours and forty-five minutes.

Q. What kind of trouble did George Hopkins get himself into at Devils Tower on October 1, 1941?
A. George Hopkins parachuted from an airplane onto the top of Devils Tower. Unfortunately for Hopkins, the rope that he intended to use to descend from the summit did not land on the tower with him.

Q. How did Hopkins get off of the tower?
A. Six days after Hopkins landed on the tower, a mountain climber named Jack Durrance, who had climbed the tower before, climbed up to Hopkins and helped him climb down.

Q. What other interesting devices were offered to remove Hopkins from the top of Devils Tower?
A. The Goodyear Tire Company offered its blimp, and the U.S. Navy offered to use a helicopter.

Q. Why wasn't the offer of the helicopter accepted?
A. At that time helicopters were considered experimental and untrustworthy.

Q. How did the town of Sundance, Wyoming, get its name?
A. The town of Sundance is located at the base of a mountain by the same name in the Black Hills area of Wyoming. The Sioux tribe held many of its religious ceremonies and dances on that mountain's summit.

Q. What was the Sioux name for Sundance Mountain?
A. It was called "Wi Wacippi Paha," which meant "Temple of the Sioux."

Q. Why won't any Shoshone Indians go to the top of Bad Medicine Butte, located in Fremont County, Wyoming?
A. The butte got its name when a Shoshone brave went to the top of the butte to scout for the enemy. His fellow braves found him dead from unknown causes, with his head resting on his folded arms. Ever since that day, the Shoshone have regarded it as a place of evil.

Q. Whose name can be found carved into the granite rock near the peak of Inyan Kara Mountain about ten miles south of Sundance?
A. Colonel George Custer carved his name there when he explored the Black Hills in 1874.

Q. What striking image does a snow patch regularly form every spring on the face of a mountain known as Ishawooa Cone near Cody, Wyoming?
A. The snow patch forms the image of a rearing horse.

Q. What does the quality of the horse formation tell about the weather of the area?
A. When the horse is well formed and its reins are visible, most of the spring run-off has passed.

Q. How did Sisters Hill in Johnson County, Wyoming, get its name?
A. The hill was named after two brothers whose last name was Sister.

Q. What did a lost sheepherder named S. M. Covey vow to create if he survived a blizzard in the middle of the Red Desert in the 1890s?
A. Covey vowed to create a rest stop for travelers in the middle of the desert. He did survive the blizzard and eventually created a rest area in the desert of Sweetwater County. The rest stop is known as Little America. It has grown into a huge conglomeration of hotels, restaurants, and shops.

Q. Why was it named Little America?
A. The rest stop was named after Admiral Byrd's base camp of Little America in Antarctica. After his ordeal in the blizzard, Covey felt a kinship with Admiral Byrd.

Q. What is a jackalope?
A. A jackalope is a mythical creature with the body of a jackrabbit and the antlers of a deer.

Q. What Wyoming city is designated as the Jackalope Capital of the World?
A. Douglas, Wyoming.

Q. Does much gambling go on in Atlantic City, Wyoming?
A. No, Atlantic City is a ghost town that was the site of a gold rush in 1868. It is located thirty miles south of Lander, Wyoming. (Gambling is not legal in Wyoming.)

Q. Is there anyone to welcome you in Welcome, Wyoming?
A. No, both Welcome and nearby Mineral Hill are ghost towns ear Sundance.

Q. What nasty surprise did the residents of Lavoye, Wyoming, receive in 1924?
A. All the residents received eviction notices from the Natrona County sheriff. The Ohio Oil Company owned the land that the town was located on and wished to drill for oil beneath the site. Buildings were jacked up onto wheels and rolled to a new town site a few miles away.

Q. Does the new town of Lavoye exist today?
A. No, it is a ghost town.

Q. What is strange about the flow of water through Swift Creek, a small stream near Afton?
A. Swift Creek is fed by the world's largest periodic spring. A periodic spring discharges its flow for short periods of time and the stops, only to resume flowing a few minutes later.

Q. How often does the flow of the Periodic Spring go through its cycle in twenty-four hours?
A. The cycle varies according to the time of year and local precipitation, but it generally cycles from full flow to dry bed every four to twenty-five minutes.

Q. How much water gushes out of the Periodic Spring on a good flow?
A. The Periodic Spring can discharge 285 gallons a second, or about ten bathtubs of water. It actually makes a roaring sound as it rises to the spring mouth.

Q. What domestic household fixture best explains how the Periodic Spring works?
A. The Periodic Spring works like a toilet bowl in reverse. The "bowl" is a reservoir buried within the rock behind the spring. When water in the reservoir reaches a certain level, it "flushes" through siphon action to the spring opening and into the streambed.

Q. Where can a visitor witness a river's disappearance into a cave in a canyon wall, only to see the river reappear in a huge spring pool one-quarter mile downstream?

A. Sinks Canyon State Park near Lander is where the Popo Agie River "sinks" beneath a canyon wall and reappears one-quarter mile below.

Q. What is the name of the pool where the river reemerges?
A. The pool is called "The Rise," of course.

Q. How much water flows through this invisible stretch of the Popo Agic River?
A. Depending upon the time of year, 150 to 500 cubic feet of water per second flow into the sink and back out the rise.

Q. Has anyone explored the underground path of the stream?
A. No, but dye tests have proven the same water exits the underground channels that enters above.

Q. How long does the water take to traverse this underground quarter mile?
A. The dye tests prove that the journey requires two hours.

Q. Is some water lost in the path underground?
A. No, the amount of water actually increases when the river emerges at the Rise.

Q. What does Popo Agie mean?
A. It is a Crow Indian name meaning "Tall Grass River." Tall clumps of wild rye grass grow along the banks of the river.

Q. What is unique about Bear River in Uinta County, Wyoming?
A. Bear River is the longest river in the western hemisphere that does not reach an ocean. It meanders more than 500 miles through Wyoming, Idaho, and Utah before entering the Great Salt Lake.

Q. What man has more Wyoming places named after him than any other man?
A. The mountain man, Jim Bridger, has more than twenty places in Wyoming named for him.

Q. What Native American has at least eleven Wyoming locations named for him?

A. Chief Washakie of the Shoshone Indians has at least eleven places named for him in Wyoming, including a county, a mountain, a national forest, a lake, and a town.

Q. Although he was given a large, fine house on the reservation in Wyoming, Chief Washakie usually stayed in a tepee instead. What did Washakie use the house for?
A. He stabled his favorite horse there.

Q. What does the word "Washakie" mean?
A. It means "rattler" in Shoshone. The name refers to the turtle shell rattle that Chief Washakie used when dancing.

Q. How many places in Wyoming start with the words "Dead Man"?
A. At least twelve places in Wyoming have names starting with the words "Dead Man," including three different Dead Man Gulches.

Q. How many places in Wyoming start with the word "Devil's"? (Hint: the answer is an unlucky number.)
A. Thirteen places start with the word "Devil's", including three Devil's Kitchens.

Q. How did Man-Eater Canyon in Converse County, Wyoming, get its name?
A. A man named Alferd Packer was apprehended here in 1883 to be extradited to Colorado. Packer, a prospector, had supposedly killed and eaten five of his partners.

Q. Did Alferd Packer commit his crimes in Wyoming?
A. No, he committed the crimes in Colorado and was jailed in Saguache, Colorado. He escaped from prison there in 1874, but was apprehended again, nine years later, in Cheyenne.

Q. Where did the town of Newcastle, Wyoming, get its name?
A. The Wyoming town was named after the town of Newcastle-Upon-Tyne, England. Newcastle-Upon-Tyne was a port city for Northern England's coal. Newcastle was a railroad terminal for Wyoming's coal.

Q. Is coal still the major export from Newcastle, Wyoming?
A. No, oil has surpassed coal as the most important export.

Q. What was unique about one of Newcastle's first oil wells?
A. When some locals attempted to dig a water well, they struck oil instead.

Q. Tubb Town is a ghost town located near Newcastle. Its residents relocated to Newcastle to be near the railroad. How did one Tubb Town bar owner keep his business going while he moved?
A. He sold drinks from his bar as he hauled it by wagon from Tubb Town to Newcastle.

Q. How much salt is in the water from Salt Springs, Wyoming?
A. The water contains three quarters of a pound of salt per gallon of water, or about 10 percent of volume.

Q. How much salt is contained in an average gallon of seawater?
A. A gallon of seawater contains about one quarter of a pound of salt or about 3.5 percent of volume.

Q. What was the salt used for in the 1880s?
A. The salt was made into salt lick blocks for cattle and horses, in Deadwood, South Dakota.

Q. How did Brokenback Creek in the Bighorn Basin get its name?
A. A wagon broke down while crossing the creek. A man tried to repair the wagon but it collapsed on him. Although his back was not broken, the man was injured and the stream has been known as Brokenback Creek ever since.

Q. What two towns in Wyoming were the first in the entire northwestern region of the United States to have natural gas-powered lights and heat?
A. In 1910, the neighboring towns of Basin and Greybull both received the first natural gas utilities in the Northwest.

Q. What is the largest lake in Wyoming?
A. Yellowstone Lake in Yellowstone National Park is the largest lake in Wyoming.

Q. How many square miles are covered by the surface of Yellowstone Lake?
A. Yellowstone Lake covers 136 square miles.

Q. Lake De Smet, near Buffalo, Wyoming, was named after its discoverer, Catholic missionary Father Pierre Jean De Smet. What was the Sioux name for the lake?
A. The Sioux called it Medicine Lake.

Q. What did Sioux and Cheyenne warriors use the lake for?
A. The warriors, including Crazy Horse, often went there on vision quests, seeking guidance from their spirit helpers.

Q. Where can a visitor shout out his or her name and hear it echoed back to them at least three times?
A. A visitor can stand on the edge of the Bighorn River Canyon just north of Lovell, Wyoming, and shout out his name, hearing it echoed back three times.

Q. How deep is the Bighorn River Canyon at its deepest point?
A. The deepest point is 2,200 feet below the canyon rim.

Q. How long is Bighorn Lake, which extends up the Bighorn River Canyon from the Yellowtail Dam in Montana?
A. The lake is 71 miles long. It floods 55 miles of the floor of the Bighorn River Canyon.

Q. What jurisdiction controls the area of Bighorn Lake?
A. Bighorn Lake is part of the Bighorn Canyon National Recreation Area, and is controlled by the National Park Service.

Q. How many lakes are named Lake Solitude in Wyoming?
A. Three: one is located in the Cloud Peak Wilderness of the Big Horn Mountains, one is located in the Teton Mountains, and another is located in the Glacier Primitive Area of Fremont County.

Q. What dam on the Platte River was built entirely by human and animal labor from 1905 to 1909?
A. The Pathfinder Dam, named after the western explorer John Charles "Pathfinder" Fremont, was built using horse-drawn graders and hand-quarried stone. The dam is 218 feet high and 432 feet long. It forms a lake containing 1,016,000 acre-feet of water. This is about enough water for the population of Los Angeles for one year.

Q. What was the tallest dam in the world in 1910?
A. The Buffalo Bill Dam, just a couple of miles west of Cody on the Shoshone River, was the tallest dam in the world upon its completion in 1910.

Q. How tall is the Buffalo Bill Dam?
A. The Buffalo Bill Dam is 328 feet tall.

Q. Where is the highest dam in the world today?
A. The Rogun Dam in Tajikistan is currently the highest dam in the world at 1,100 feet in height

Q. Heart Mountain resembles a heart when viewed from Powell, Wyoming. What does it resemble when viewed from Cody, Wyoming?
A. The mountain is commonly said to resemble a reclining Indian with one knee raised, or an Indian's profile looking toward the sky, with a wart on his chin.

Q. How long has Heart Mountain been known by this name?
A. While it is uncertain how long the Indians used this name for the distinctive mountain, the name appears on Lewis and Clark maps. Lewis and Clark never visited the mountain, but John Colter, a member of their expedition and one of the first known white men into the Wyoming territory, did view the mountain.

Q. What is the name of a nearby pass that separates the Absaroka and Beartooth Mountains?
A. The pass is named Dead Indian Pass.

Q. What is the highest peak in Wyoming?
A. Gannett Peak in the Wind River Mountains is the highest peak in Wyoming.

Q. How high is Gannett Peak?
A. Gannett Peak is 13,804 feet in elevation.

Q. Of the highest points in each state, where does Gannett Peak rank in the difficulty of climbing?
A. Gannett Peak is ranked second in difficulty of ascent, surpassed only by Denali in Alaska.

Q. How many days does the ascent of Gannett Peak usually require?
A. The total trip usually requires four to six days. The actual approach to the base of the mountain, on horseback or on foot from a highway, is more than forty miles. This is longer than the approach to Denali.

Q. What is unique about Gannett Glacier on Gannett Peak?
A. It is considered to be the largest glacier in the Lower 48 states.

Q. Is Gannett Glacier the only glacier on Gannett Peak?
A. No, at least three other glaciers are located upon the mountain.

Q. Who is Gannett Peak named after?
A. The mountain is named in honor of the American geographer, Henry Gannett. He was president of the National Geographic Society from 1910 to 1914.

Q. Where is the lowest point in Wyoming?
A. The lowest point is 3,100 feet above sea level on the Belle Fourche River near Devil's Tower.

Q. Who actually laid out the first general plan for the route of the Union Pacific Railroad through the Rocky Mountains of Wyoming?
A. The mountain man Jim Bridger used a piece of charcoal from his campfire to draw the route for railroad engineers. He traced a route through the southern part of Wyoming.

Q. How much land did the Union Pacific Railroad receive to build its tracks across Wyoming?

A. The Union Pacific railroad received 20 sections of land for every mile of track that it laid.

Q. How big is a section?
A. A section is one square mile, or 640 acres.

Q. Were the sections arranged in one continuous chunk?
A. No, the sections were arranged in a checkerboard pattern along either side of the tracks.

Q. Does the Union Pacific Railroad still own this land?
A. Most of the land was sold to the cattle barons in the 1880s or turned over to the Bureau of Land Management (BLM) because no one wanted to buy it.

Q. Was that the only compensation received by the Union Pacific to build its railroad?
A. No, the Union Pacific received additional subsidies from the federal government for each mile of track. The UP received $16,000 per mile to a point just west of Cheyenne, $48,000 per mile to cross the following 150 miles of the Great Divide, and $32,000 per mile for any additional track beyond the Divide.

Q. How did the town of Rawlins get its name?
A. A railroad surveyor named General John A. Rawlins discovered a spring of water at the site of the future town and wished it to be named after him. He was a Civil War veteran and the railroad owned the land, so his friend General Dodge, the lead railroad engineer, named the town for him.

Q. What is significant about a lone pine tree growing out of a granite boulder near Laramie, which is now surrounded by a protective fence?
A. General Grenville Dodge, the chief engineer for the Union Pacific Railroad in 1865, was surveying a path for the railroad when he and his party were attacked by Indians. They fled down the pass containing this very tree and made a mental note of it as a marker for a future path over the mountains.

Q. Where was the first Intercontinental Missile Base established in the United States?
A. It was established at Warren Air Force Base in Cheyenne, Wyoming.

Q. When were the missiles installed?
A. The installation began in 1960.

Q. How many missile silos does Warren Air Force Base control?
A. It services 200 Minuteman III missile silos. It is the largest missile wing in the free world. The sizes of missile bases in communist or socialist countries cannot be ascertained.

SCIENCE AND NATURE

Q. What is the coldest recorded temperature in Wyoming?
A. A negative 66 degrees Fahrenheit was recorded at the Riverside rest stop in central Wyoming on February 9, 1933.

Q. What was the hottest recorded temperature in Wyoming?
A. 115 degrees Fahrenheit was recorded in Basin on July 12, 1900.

Q. What was the greatest amount of rain to fall in Wyoming in one day?
A. 6.06 inches of rain fell in Cheyenne on August 1, 1985.

Q. What was the largest amount of snow to fall in Wyoming in a single day?
A. 38 inches of snow fell at Burgess Junction in the Bighorn Mountains on March 14, 1973.

Q. What is the Wyoming State Mammal?
A. The American bison, *Bison bison*, is the Wyoming state mammal.

Q. What other state has the bison as its state mammal?
A. Oklahoma.

Q. How did bison block trains when railroad tracks were first laid across Wyoming?
A. During bad weather bison herds sought shelter in the long, deep excavations where the railroad grade cut through hills. The bison herds were so dense in the narrow cuts that trains could not pass.

Q. Which way do bison face during winter storms: into the wind or away from the wind?
A. Bison face into the wind because their fur is much thicker on the front portion of their bodies and they can better scent approaching danger. Domestic cattle put their tails to the wind.

Q. How long is the hair on a bison's forehead?
A. The hair is 16 inches long.

Q. How fast can bison run?
A. 45 miles an hour.

Q. Can bison swim?
A. Yes, they swim very well. They float so well that their bodies rise almost halfway out of the water.

Q. Which is more dangerous, a bison or a black bear?
A. Nothing is more dangerous in Wyoming than a bison. Four times as many people have been killed or injured by bison in Yellowstone National Park than have been killed or injured by bears. Fifty-six people have been injured by bison in the park.

Q. Was the bison confined only to the West?
A. In Colonial times bison roamed from the Atlantic coast nearly to the Pacific. They did not exist in such large numbers in the eastern states as in the West, but they were common. Buffalo, New York, was named for the herds there, although the name is derived from the original place name given the area by local Seneca Indians.

Q. What is the largest land mammal in Wyoming?
A. The bison is the largest, weighing more than a ton.

Q. Bison have horns. What is horn made of?
A. Horn is a true boney extension that is permanent. Horns are never shed, while antlers are shed seasonally.

Q. Which sex of bison has horns?
A. Both cow and bull bison have horns.

Q. Which is more nutritious, bison meat or beef?
A. Bison meat has 70 percent less fat and 30 percent more protein than beef. It has nearly 60 percent less cholesterol than beef.

Q. How long do bison live?
A. A bison may live for 40 years.

Q. Before the white man arrived with firearms, how many bison existed in North America?
A. Between 30 and 60 million bison roamed from Alaska to Mexico and from the east to the west coasts.

Q. How wide was an average bison herd's range of travel?
A. 200 miles.

Q. What effect did railroads entering the West have on the bison herds?
A. The effect was devastating. Multitudes of gun-bearing market hunters arrived. The railroads hauled away the hides of nearly all of the bison in ten years. Only a few thousand remained scattered in remote areas and national parks.

Q. When were the most bison killed by hide hunters in Wyoming?
A. From 1873 to 1878.

Q. Approximately how many bison were killed in Wyoming during the 1870s?
A. 12 million.

Q. What was the value of a bison hide in the mid-1870s?
A. $3.50.

Q. Other than coats and robes, what other uses were bison hides prized for?
A. They were made into large belts for driving the new machinery of the Industrial Age. Many of the hides were sent to Europe for this purpose.

Q. After the bison herds were decimated, what other bison product did people gather from the plains to sell?
A. People gathered bison bones for several years after the great herds were gone, to grind up for fertilizer.

Q. What was the value of ground bison bone?
A. $5.00 a pound.

Q. What other purpose was bison bone used for?
A. It was used in the manufacturing of bone china. Bone china is the finest and most durable variety of china.

Q. How many different wildlife species inhabit Wyoming?
A. 604.

Q. What branch of the mammal kingdom are badgers a member of?
A. Badgers are members of the weasel family.

Q. How much does a badger weigh?
A. A badger may weigh as much as thirty pounds.

Q. How do badgers hunt for prey?
A. Badgers dig for mice, voles, prairie dogs and other burrow-dwelling creatures.

Q. How fast can a badger dig a hole to hide itself?
A. Digging with all four feet, a badger can go completely underground in a minute and a half.

Q. What other common predator do badgers sometimes team up with when hunting?
A. Badgers and coyotes sometimes work together to catch prey. If the prey animal scoots out of its backdoor hole, the coyote may catch it. If the coyote hangs around above ground, then the prey stays underground where the badger can dig it up.

Q. Will badgers avoid humans?
A. Badgers are not afraid of many things, including humans. They are strong animals with powerful claws and jaws.

Q. What sacred location was often a hangout for badgers?
A. In the Old West, cemeteries were often located on high ground with poor sandy soil. These sites were often prime hunting grounds for badgers and they continued to dig there even after bodies were buried, much to the displeasure of the townspeople.

Q. What men's bathroom implement was made of badger hair?
A. Badger hair was once used to make the finest shaving brushes.

Q. How much can a large beaver weigh?
A. A beaver may weigh up to 90 pounds, but most do not weigh more than 50 pounds.

Q. Are there any species of rodents larger than beavers?
A. Only the South American capybara is larger than the American beaver.

Q. What body part of a beaver grows about an inch a month?
A. A beaver's teeth grow about one inch a month. They also wear down about an inch a month from the beaver's constant gnawing of wood.

Q. Other than trapping by humans, what is one of the leading causes of death among beavers?
A. Beavers are often killed by the falling trees that they have gnawed through while feeding.

Q. How many rooms does a beaver lodge contain?
A. A beaver lodge often has two rooms. The first is where the beaver dries off after emerging from the underwater entrance; the second room is the actual living space.

Q. How does a beaver signal other beavers that danger is near?
A. A threatened beaver will slap its tail on the surface of the water with a loud "smack" as it dives beneath the water to escape.

Q. What dubious honor did the Roman Catholic Church bestow upon the beaver in the 1600s?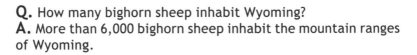
A. In response to the Bishop of Quebec, the Pope categorized beaver as fish so that beaver meat could be eaten on Fridays during Lent.

Q. How many bighorn sheep inhabit Wyoming?
A. More than 6,000 bighorn sheep inhabit the mountain ranges of Wyoming.

Q. How much do Rocky Mountain bighorn sheep weigh?
A. Rams can weigh more than 300 pounds and ewes weigh around 200 pounds.

Q. How much do the horns of a large bighorn ram weigh?
A. The horns may weigh 40 pounds, about the same weight as all the other bones in the ram's skeleton.

Q. What did the Shoshone and Sheepeater Indians create from the horns of bighorn rams?
A. Powerful bows were created from laminations of the horns and wood.

Q. Are all black bears black?
A. No, black bears come in a variety of colors, from black through various shades of brown, to nearly blonde. Some have white blazes on their chests.

Q. How large do black bears get?
A. Mature black bears weigh between 100 and 500 pounds.

Q. What is unusual about a black bear's gait in comparison to the gait most of the rest of mammals?
A. A black bear moves both feet on one side of its body at the same time, instead of moving feet on the opposite sides at the same time as most other species of mammal do.

Q. Black bears utilize embryonic diapause to ensure a good start to the development of their cubs. What is embryonic diapause?

A. Although black bears breed in the middle to late summer months, the embryos do not begin to develop until the mother bear goes into hibernation in November or December. This delay is called embryonic diapause.

Q. What happens to a black bear's paws during hibernation?
A. The old foot pad surface sheds off and a fresh new one takes its place.

Q. Black bears rarely attack humans, unless protecting their young or pursuing handouts. Why is it unwise to play dead when attacked by a black bear?
A. Grizzly bears attack humans for defensive purposes. While black bears rarely attack, on the rare occasions that they have attacked, it has been in a predatory fashion. In other words, they wish to eat the victim.

Q. In 1974, the black-footed ferret was regarded as extinct. Where was a remaining colony of black-footed ferrets discovered in 1981?
A. A rancher's dog killed a black-footed ferret near Meeteetse, Wyoming, leading to the discovery of the remaining colony of black-footed ferrets.

Q. How many ferrets existed in this remaining colony?
A. 130 ferrets existed in the colony, but disease reduced the number to 13. These last 13 were trapped and the species was reestablished in captivity. Black-footed ferrets are still highly endangered, but several new wild colonies have been established in Wyoming and other western states.

Q. How can an observer tell a bobcat from a lynx?
A. Lynxes are usually bigger than bobcats. A bobcat has a black tip on its stubby tail. A lynx's tail is white underneath, with no black tip.

Q. Bobcats are crepuscular. What does this mean?
A. Crepuscular means that they are most active during the hours around dawn and dusk and less active during full darkness or full daylight.

Q. How much does a bobcat weigh?
A. A large male bobcat may weigh over 30 pounds. Bobcats are about twice as large as the average house cat.

Q. What is a coyote's main food source?
A. A coyote eats rodents for most of its diet.

Q. What great benefit do humans add to a coyote's diet in the fall and early winter each year?
A. Hunters provide large amounts of fresh meat for coyotes each year when they clean their deer, elk and other game.

Q. How many different calls do coyotes make while howling?
A. Coyote biologists have distinguished at least eleven different calls.

Q. How fast can coyotes run?
A. Coyotes can run forty miles per hour.

Q. What is a coydog?
A. A coydog is a hybrid animal created when coyotes and dogs interbreed. Coyotes can also interbreed with wolves.

Q. What is the survival rate for coyote pups in the first year of their lives?
A. Only 5 to 20 percent of coyote pups survive their first year of life.

Q. How high can coyotes jump?
A. Coyotes have been observed jumping over eight-foot fences.

Q. What is the Wyoming State Fish?
A. The cutthroat trout.

Q. What is the only trout species native to the Rocky mountain region?
A. The cutthroat trout is the only species native to Wyoming and the Rocky Mountain region.

Q. How many cutthroat trout subspecies exist in Wyoming?
A. Wyoming has four native cutthroat trout species swimming within its waters: the Yellowstone, Snake, Bonneville, and Colorado River varieties. These are more subspecies than found in any other state.

Q. Are golden eagles found only in North America?
A. No, golden eagles are found on all continents of the Northern Hemisphere.

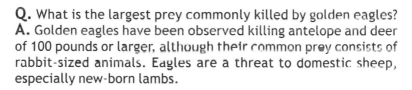

Q. Do golden eagles mate for life?
A. Yes.

Q. What is the largest prey commonly killed by golden eagles?
A. Golden eagles have been observed killing antelope and deer of 100 pounds or larger, although their common prey consists of rabbit-sized animals. Eagles are a threat to domestic sheep, especially new-born lambs.

Q. Do bald eagles scream when they call?
A. No, their call is more like a shrill squeak. The call often heard in movies is the call of the red-tailed hawk dubbed over the eagle's natural, less noble call.

Q. Is anyone allowed to possess eagle feathers?
A. Only people of certified Native American descent are allowed to possess eagle feathers. The feathers may be used for religious purposes only.

Q. What hawk species, native to Wyoming, may often be confused with immature golden eagles?
A. The ferruginous hawk is large enough to resemble a young eagle and its coloration also resembles that of a young golden or bald eagle. The ferruginous hawk has light-colored comma markings beneath its wings and feathered legs. DNA testing has suggested the possibility of classifying the ferruginous hawk as an eagle.

Q. Does an osprey catch a fish on every dive that it makes?
A. No, an osprey catches a fish about every second try.

Q. How much does a bald eagle weigh?
A. A bald eagle weighs about twelve pounds.

Q. What is the Native American name for elk?
A. Wapiti.

Q. What animal do Europeans refer to as elk?
A. Europeans refer to moose as elk.

Q. How many elk inhabit Wyoming?
A. Over 100,000 elk live in Wyoming.

Q. How much does a large bull elk weigh?
A. A large bull elk may weigh over 800 pounds.

Q. How much does a large set of elk antlers weigh?
A. A large set of elk antlers may weigh more than forty pounds.

Q. How fast do elk antlers grow?
A. They can grow at the rate of one inch per day.

Q. Why do elk bugle?
A. Bull elk bugle, or make a high piercing modulated call, in the early fall to attract a mate and to challenge rival bulls.

Q. About how many grizzly bears inhabit Wyoming?
A. Grizzly bears are difficult to count, but the best estimate is about 600 bears.

Q. Does a grizzly bear get its name from the grisly eating habits?
A. No, "grizzly" is short for "grizzled" or grayed, in reference to the adult grizzly's silver-tipped fur.

Q. How much does an average grizzly bear from Wyoming weigh?
A. 500 pounds.

Q. How much does a Wyoming grizzly's cousin, an Alaskan Kodiak Island brown bear, weigh?
A. More than 1,200 pounds.

Q. If a healthy grizzly bear eats thirty-five pounds of food a week, how much weight does it gain in a week?
A. A grizzly bear may gain forty pounds a week and double its weight by hibernation time in the fall.

Q. What do biologists examine on a bear to decisively determine its age?
A. Biologists may pull or drill a bear's tooth to count the growth rings within. Each ring represents one year, just as with a tree's growth rings.

Q. How many teeth does a bear have?
A. Forty-two, ten more than a human.

Q. One of the distinguishing characteristics between a grizzly bear and a black bear is the grizzly bear's hump on its shoulders. What is this hump made of?
A. The hump is made of muscle to power the grizzly's forepaws.

Q. Do grizzly bears only eat meat?
A. No, grizzly bears are omnivores. This means that they eat plant life as well as other animals. Bears dig up roots and eat berries, fruits, seeds, nuts, and grass. They eat rodents much more often than elk, deer, and moose calves. Seldom do they eat a full-grown elk or deer.

Q. Do grizzly bears eat bugs?
A. Yes, quite often. They are particularly fond of army cutworm moths, which gather on high mountain rock slides in the warm summer sun. Bears spend all day turning over rocks to gobble up the moths, as many as 40,000 moths a day per bear.

Q. Do biologists know why the bears like these moths for dinner so well?
A. Yes, the moths possess the highest calorie value for their weight of any of the bears' food sources.

Q. What rare high-altitude tree is important to the grizzly bear's diet?
A. Grizzly bears derive a large portion of their winter fat reserves from the nuts in white bark pine cones.

Q. How long are a grizzly bear's claws?
A. The longest are over four inches long.

Q. Are bears true hibernators, sleeping through the entire winter without ever waking up?
A. No, bears actually will wake up at various times during the winter.

Q. A bear's normal heart rate is about 50 beats per minute. What is its heart rate during hibernation?
A. The bear's heart rate will slow to about 10 beats per minute.

Q. What has the recent arrival of wolves to Wyoming done to the hibernation patterns of bears in areas where the two animals coexist?
A. Bears are waking up more often to feed on the leftovers of the wolf kills.

Q. How fast can a grizzly run?
A. A lot faster than a human; a bear can run 35 to 40 miles an hour.

Q. How long does a grizzly bear live?
A. A grizzly bear may live for thirty years.

Q. Can grizzly bears climb trees?
A. Grizzly bears cannot climb trees with their claws alone, as a cat would. They are very agile at climbing from limb to limb on bigger trees.

Q. How frequently do female grizzlies (sows) give birth?
A. Grizzly sows give birth to one or two cubs every other year on average. Triplet cubs are sometimes born in years of abundant food.

Q. If very rich cow milk contains four percent fat, how much fat does grizzly bear milk contain?
A. Grizzly bear milk is almost 50 percent fat in content.

Q. How good are a cub's chances of survival to adulthood?
A. A cub's chances of survival are little better than fifty-fifty. Only three out of five cubs survive into their second year of life.

Q. How far can a jack rabbit jump horizontally?
A. 20 feet.

Q. Are there any lynx in Wyoming?
A. Yes, a very few. Some have been reintroduced into Colorado and have wandered north, while others have traveled south from Canada and Montana. Bobcats are much more common.

Q. Which is larger; a lynx or a bobcat?
A. Lynx weigh from 30 to 60 pounds, while bobcats rarely exceed 30 pounds. Lynx have very large feet and look as if they are walking in oversized pajamas. Bobcats are more streamlined in appearance.

Q. How much does a moose weigh?
A. A moose can weigh over 1,000 pounds. It is the largest member of the deer family.

Q. How long can a moose keep its head submerged?
A. A moose can keep its head submerged for three minutes

Q. Why would a moose wish to keep its head underwater for three minutes?
A. Underwater plants make up a large part of a moose's diet during the summer months of the year. They eat bark and twigs during the frozen winter months.

Q. How much does a large set of moose antlers weigh?
A. A pair of large antlers may weigh ninety pounds or more.

Q. Have moose always existed in Wyoming?
A. Archeological evidence suggests that moose did not migrate into Wyoming until the early 1800s. No one is certain why this is so.

Q. Do billy or nanny mountain goats have horns?
A. Both billy and nanny mountain goats have true horns, although the billy, or male, mountain goats have longer horns.

Q. What is unique about the hooves of mountain goats?
A. The inner portion of the hoof is soft, like a very flexible sneaker sole, to aid in climbing.

Q. How large are mountain goats?
A. A big male will stand over three feet at the shoulder and weigh over two hundred pounds.

Q. Are mountain lions endangered in Wyoming?
A. No, Wyoming has a very healthy population of mountain lions. The big cat is extremely elusive, so most people have not seen one in the wild, even though they may be nearby.

Q. Are mountain lions dangerous to humans?
A. Mountain lions generally avoid human contact, but they may also show little fear of humans if encountered in the wilderness. Small children and adults of slight build could be at risk in times of scant food for a mountain lion, or when it feels threatened. Pets are always at some risk in lion country.

Q. Are mountain lions hunted in Wyoming?
A. Yes, they are hunted. This also seems to reinforce their fear of human contact in many areas.

Q. How much does an adult male mountain lion weigh?
A. A male mountain lion may weigh over 150 pounds. Females weigh somewhat less.

Q. How much weight can a mountain lion drag?
A. A mountain lion can drag a kill seven times heavier than itself.

Q. How many kittens are born to a mountain lion mother?
A. Three to four kittens are born each year to adult female mountain lions.

Q. Are there more mule deer or people in Wyoming?
A. The count is about even at half a million for each species. If whitetail deer are added in, the deer population is greater by about 100,000.

Q. What unusual seashore bird can be sighted often along the rivers and lakes of Wyoming?
A. The pelican can.

Q. How many quills does an average porcupine have?
A 30,000 quills.

Q. How much does a large porcupine weigh?
A. A full-grown porcupine can weigh forty-five pounds.

Q. Wyoming is home to 70 percent of the world's population of this large animal. What is it?
A. 70 percent of the world's pronghorn antelope live in Wyoming. There are over 400,000 roaming the state's grasslands.

Q. How fast can a pronghorn run?
A. The pronghorn can run over 60 miles per hour, making it the second fastest land animal in the world, second only to the cheetah.

Q. What man-made barrier now threatens pronghorn antelope?
A. Livestock fences, both barbed wire and woven wire sheep fences, severely inhibit movements of pronghorn antelope for water and forage. Pronghorns do not jump over fences. They will crawl under the bottom wire on a strand fence, if it is high enough. Highway barrier fences also deter pronghorn migrations.

Q. Do pronghorn antelope have horns or antlers?
A. Pronghorn antelope have true horns. The antelope horn is composed of a black sheath made of keratin enclosing a permanent boney inner core. The sheath is shed every year.

Q. Which gender of pronghorn has horns?
A. Both sexes have horns, although the female's horns are not easily seen.

Q. What property of the pronghorn's fur makes it a good insulator for the bitter Wyoming winters?
A. The hair is hollow, making it a superior insulator.

Q. How good is a pronghorn's vision?
A. A pronghorn has eyesight comparable to 8x binoculars and the

pronghorn has a field of vision of nearly a complete circle.

Q. Pronghorns are often called "goats" by local people. Are they related to goats?
A. No, pronghorns are not true antelope, nor are they related to goats. Pronghorns are a unique species with no closely related species in the animal kingdom.

Q. What slender, weasel-like mammal may be seen hunting squirrels in the forests of Wyoming?
A. The American marten hunts squirrels and birds among the treetops of Wyoming forests. It is related to the European sable.

Q. What do martens have in common with cats?
A. Martens can retract their claws as cats can.

Q. What is the large silvery-colored mammal found commonly in the high mountains of Wyoming?
A. The marmot is often seen above treeline in the mountains of Wyoming. The large rodent will often whistle in alarm if it is approached by humans.

Q. What tiny, squeaking animal might a person see scurrying from boulder to boulder on a high mountain rock slide?
A. The pika is a small mammal that inhabits high alpine rock slides.

Q. Is the pika related to mice or voles?
A. The pika is not related to mice or voles. It is a close relative to rabbits and hares.

Q. Does a pika hibernate?
A. No, pikas stay active beneath the snow all winter.

Q. What do pikas and ranchers have in common?
A. Pikas, like ranchers, make hay in the summer months by cutting grasses and piling them in the sun to dry. When the hay is dry, it is stored beneath the rocks in and around their burrows for use during the winter.

Q. Why are pikas often seen fighting with each other?
A. Pikas are terrible thieves, often stealing each other's hay stash and getting caught at the crime.

Q. Why are prairie dogs called dogs?
A. The warning call of prairie dogs sounds like the bark of a small dog.

Q. How large can prairie dog towns be?
A. Prairie dog towns may extend over several hundred acres and contain several hundred animals.

Q. How deep do prairie dog tunnels go?
A. Tunnels may drop 17 feet into the ground and extend horizontally 30 feet or more with several branching chambers.

Q. What large gray bird, standing nearly five feet tall on long spindly legs, with a long neck and red skull cap, is a common sight in Wyoming in the summer months?
A. The sandhill crane is a common summer resident to much of Wyoming. The bird gives a deep, rattling call that carries over long distances. Its call is a sure sign of spring.

Q. What ancient fish species is found in small numbers in the Powder River of northeastern Wyoming?
A. The shovelnose sturgeon is a two- to three-foot primitive fish found in the Powder River. Caviar is extracted from its larger cousins in Europe and Asia.

Q. What is the smallest wild dog, or canid, in North America today?
A. The swift fox is the smallest species of wild dog in North America today. About the size of an average housecat, it exists in small numbers in Wyoming.

Q. Is an average person traveling through Wyoming likely to see a swift fox?
A. Even though large portions of Wyoming are suitable habitat for swift foxes, the little tan and gray creatures are mostly nocturnal and not out hunting during daylight hours.

Q. Why are they called swift foxes?
A. The little foxes with big ears are extremely quick for their size, darting around at speeds of 40 miles an hour.

Q. What weather condition do swift foxes dislike?
A. Swift foxes dislike windy weather and will usually remain in their dens.

Q. What is the wingspan of a trumpeter swan?
A. Trumpeter swans have a wingspan of eight feet to support their thirty-pound weight.

Q. How much does a trumpeter swan eat in a day?
A. A trumpeter swan eats nearly two thirds of its body weight or about twenty pounds of aquatic plants a day.

Q. What percentage of a trumpeter swan's total body length is made up of its neck?
A. Nearly half of the swan's length is composed of its neck.

Q. Do swans dive for food?
A. No, they reach down with their long necks beneath the water's surface to feed.

Q. How many trumpeter swans existed in the world in 1932?
A. Sixty-nine trumpeter swans were all that remained in 1932, after market hunters had killed them for their magnificent plumes and their meat.

Q. How are trumpeter swans distinguished from more common mute swans, whooper swans, or tundra swans?
A. Mute swans, tundra swans, and whooper swans have orange or yellow on their bills. Trumpeter swans have black bills.

Q. How large do wolverines get?
A. Wolverines may weigh as much as 55 pounds and be over three feet long. Female wolverines are only two thirds the size of male wolverines.

Q. Are wolverines found only in North America?
A. No, wolverines also inhabit extreme Northern Europe and Russia.

Q. Wolverines are sometimes called "skunk bear" and "nasty cat." Why?
A. Wolverines, being a member of the weasel family, often give off a very nasty odor.

Q. Wolverines are known for their ferocious nature. What is the largest prey that a wolverine has been witnessed killing?
A. Wolverines have been observed on a few rare occasions killing moose. The moose was either severely weakened or stuck in deep snow at the time.

Q. How large is a wolverine's territory?
A. A male wolverine may roam a home territory of 240 square miles.

Q. When were wolves reintroduced into Yellowstone National Park?
A. Thirty-one wolves from Canada were reintroduced into Yellowstone in 1995.

Q. How many wolves exist in Wyoming today?
A. Approximately 250.

Q. How much meat per day does a wolf require?
A. A wolf must eat at least four pounds of meat per day to maintain good condition.

Q. What is the Wyoming State Flower?
A. The Indian paintbrush (*Castilleja linariaefolia*).

Q. How many other states use the Indian paintbrush as their state flower?
A. None; Wyoming is the only one.

Q. What is another common name for the Indian paintbrush?
A. Prairie fire is another name.

Q. In the Indian legend that gave the Indian paintbrush its name, what was the Indian warrior painting before he left his brushes scattered across the landscape?
A. He was painting the colors of the sunset.

Q. What characteristic does the Indian paintbrush exhibit that might not be considered an admirable quality?
A. The plant is semi-parasitic, usually attaching its roots to those of nearby grasses to steal nutrients and water.

Q. What is the name of the award given annually to children's books by the Wyoming Library Association and chosen by children in grades 4 through 6?
A. The Indian Paintbrush Book Award.

Q. What is the source of the snow-like substance seen floating in the air in great quantities in Wyoming in June and July?
A. The white substance is composed of seeds from the Wyoming state tree, the plains cottonwood or *Populus sargentii*.

Q. Which gender of cottonwood tree produces the cotton seed?
A. Only female trees produce the clouds of cotton seed.

Q. How old do cottonwood trees get to be?
A. Although cottonwood trees are often very large, this because they are very fast growing. Trees do not usually live much beyond seventy to one hundred years.

Q. Are there more or fewer cottonwood trees today than there were during pioneer times?
A. In Wyoming, more cottonwood trees exist today by far, than were present along the streams and rivers of Wyoming during pioneer days. Floods, fire, drought, and bison herds once held cottonwoods to isolated groves along the Wyoming watercourses.

Q. Is this true in urban areas of Wyoming?
A. Cottonwood numbers are in decline in many urban areas of Wyoming, as well as other western states, because the old trees become unstable and dangerous. They are cut down and usually replaced with ornamental trees.

Q. Now that water levels are controlled and the huge herds of bison are gone, what changes have occurred in the types of wildlife found in Wyoming?

A. Eastern North American species, such as the fox squirrel, have invaded the state along the cottonwood-forested corridors of the river bottoms.

Q. What use did the Native Americans have for the inner bark of young cottonwoods?
A. They used it for food for their horses in late winter or early spring, sometimes resorting to eating the sweet bark themselves in times of hardship.

Q. What is the Wyoming State Grass?
A. Western wheatgrass is the Wyoming State Grass.

Q. What useful characteristics does western wheatgrass possess to merit its designation as Wyoming's State Grass?
A. The plant is good forage for cattle and does well in high-altitude dry soils. It is a good choice for reclaiming mining areas. Wheatgrass also does well in salty or alkaline soils.

Q. What is the Wyoming State Fossil?
A. A small herring-like fish called the *Knightia* is the state fossil.

Q. Who spearheaded the effort to make the *Knightia* the state fossil in 1987?
A. Fred Hulbert, an elementary student, spoke before the State Senate and House of Representatives requesting that this honor be bestowed upon the *Knightia*.

Q. Why is this 5- to 10-inch fish called the *Knightia*?
A. It is named after the first Wyoming State Geologist, William Clinton Knight.

Q. When was this fossil fish first discovered in Wyoming?
A. *Knightia* were first seen in Wyoming in the 1840s by explorers and missionaries. Later, entire fossilized schools of the fish were unearthed by the Union Pacific Railroad as it cut railroad beds through the Green River Formation.

Q. How old are the *Knightia* fossils?
A. They are from the Eocene Era, or 50 million years old.

Q. What other creatures were found with *Knightia*?
A. Fossil boa constrictors and crocodiles were found with *Knightla*.

Q. What Wyoming city is designated as the Fossil Fish Capital of the World?
A. Kemmerer, Wyoming is the Fossil Capital of the World. It is located in the middle of the Green River Formation—a large area of fossil-bearing sedimentary rock.

Q. What national monument is located near Kemmerer, Wyoming?
A. Fossil Butte National Monument is located near Kemmerer,. It is a hill filled with *Knightia* and other fossils.

Q. What endangered species lives in the 84.4 degree Fahrenheit waters of Kendall Hot Springs near Pinedale, Wyoming?
A. A 2-inch-long fish, named the Kendall dace, lives in the warm springs and nowhere else on Earth.

Q. Who really created the Spanish Diggings near Lusk, Wyoming?
A. Prehistoric man actually began quarrying the fine-grained quartzite, agate, and jasper from the area now known as the Spanish Diggings, for material for stone tools and projectile points. American Indians continued the practice until iron was introduced.

Q. Why are these prehistoric quarries called the Spanish Diggings?
A. The first white men to discover them thought that early Spanish explorers had perhaps reached the area and dug for riches there.
Q. How far away from Wyoming have the materials from the Spanish Diggings been found?
A. Stone implements made from materials quarried in the Spanish Diggings have been found in the Ohio and Mississippi River valleys.

Q. How did these materials migrate over these distances?
A. The materials were traded from tribe to tribe.

Q. Did the Spanish conquistadors ever explore parts of Wyoming?
A. No evidence exists of their presence in Wyoming. Coronado did explore into present-day Kansas, but none of his country-men ever traveled as far north as Wyoming.

Q. What is hidden beneath a steel door at the bottom of a forty-five-foot deep pit located only a few yards from Interstate 90 just two miles from the Wyoming/South Dakota border?
A. Twenty feet of accumulated bison bones and prehistoric stone weapons and implements are beneath the protective door. This is the location of the Vole Buffalo Jump, where Native Americans drove bison over the edge of the jump to their deaths for at least five hundred years. A more developed visitor's center is pending for the site.

Q. What prehistoric structure is located on top of the Bighorn Mountains and may be comparable to Stonehenge?
A. The ancient Native American circular structure known as the Medicine Wheel is located about 45 miles east of Lovell, Wyoming on the top of the Bighorn Mountains.

Q. Why is the Medicine Wheel comparable to Stonehenge?
A. Many people believe that the Medicine Wheel was used as an astronomical observatory and calendar.

Q. Why is the structure called a Medicine Wheel?
A. The structure consists of a low circular wall or raised path of flat stones nearly eighty feet in diameter. Twenty-eight spokes composed of the same flat stones radiate out from a center cairn to the outer circle. No existing Indian tribes know the origin of the Medicine Wheel for certain. The Wheel is considered strong magic, or good medicine.

Q. What did a solar physicist named John Eddy discover buried beneath the center pile of stones?
A. He found a large stone with a hole in it suitable to place a large pole in. He surmised that people could have studied and charted the movement of the stars with such a marker.

Q. How old is the Medicine Wheel?
A. Carbon dating has placed it at eight to nine hundred years old.

Q. Can the public visit the Medicine Wheel?
A. Yes, the Medicine Wheel is found down a well-marked turn-off to the north from Highway 14A from Ranchester or Lovell, Wyoming. A visitor must walk the remaining half mile to the site. Handicapped people may be driven.

Q. What curious objects may be seen tied to the fence surrounding the Medicine Wheel, or placed on the ground beneath it?
A. Because Native Americans consider the site sacred, they often bring prayer scarves, medicine bundles, or various religious tokens to leave at the Medicine Wheel. If you visit, leave these objects alone. They are not souvenirs. Also be respectful of any religious ceremonies taking place during your visit.

Q. Is there a special manner in which a visitor should walk around the Medicine Wheel?
A. Yes, visitors should turn to the left and travel around the wheel in a clockwise direction. This is in harmony with the religious practices of the Native Americans who have utilized the Wheel for several hundred years.

Q. Is the Bighorn Medicine Wheel the only one of its kind?
A. No, there are several other, less-elaborate medicine wheels located throughout the Rocky Mountains. Many are located in Alberta, Canada.

Q. What is the elevation of the Bighorn Medicine Wheel?
A. The Wheel is located at an elevation of 9,642 feet above sea level.

Q. What is the name of the mountain that the Medicine Wheel is located on?
A. The mountain is called Medicine Mountain.

Q. What is geologically unique about Medicine Mountain?
A. It is considered a "nucleus of continent" location. One of only a dozen or so such places upon the face of the earth, the mountain consists of layers of the Earth's crust piled one on top of each other from oldest to youngest, without interruption.

Q. What is special about Medicine Mountain, even among all of the other "nuclei of continents" sites in the world?
A. The rock layers of Medicine Mountain are in reverse—oldest on top; youngest at the valley floor. The mountain structure has been completely turned over. This is not true of the mountains surrounding Medicine Mountain.

Q. How does a complete chunk of mountain range get completely turned over?
A. The Bighorn Mountains are fault-block mountains, or mountains created when pressure from plate tectonics of the Earth's crust cause fractures in the continental crust and push the resulting pieces up with the pressure. Some chunks, like Medicine Mountain, are slowly rolled over completely.

Q. What symbol, made up of piled stones, can be found on a low ridge, located to the east of Meeteetse, Wyoming?
A. A stone arrow, called the Great Arrow, is 58 feet long and 5.5 feet wide.

Q. What does the Great Arrow point to?
A. The Great Arrow points to the Medicine Wheel in the Bighorn Mountains. It was made by the same ancient people who created the Medicine Wheel.

Q. What is a medicine tree?
A. Native Americans had an ancient custom of placing large bighorn sheep horns in the crotches of trees on high mountain trails. The horns were placed on the branches in reverence to the bighorn sheep. Offerings were left at the base of the trees, perhaps for safe passage over the high passes. As time passed, the trees grew around the ram's horns.

Q. Are these medicine trees common in Wyoming?
A. No, these trees are not common anywhere. Five examples have been found in Wyoming. They can be viewed at four locations in Wyoming: Jackson, Cody, Dubois, and Casper.

Q. What is strange about the stone of Bernard Peak in western Wyoming?
A. The granite rock rings underfoot when it is walked upon.

Q. What is particularly unusual about the Colby Mammoth Site, located in the Bighorn Basin?
A. Along with the remains of seven mammoths, archeologists found Clovis spear points from the weapons of the early humans that killed the mammoths.

Q. How old is this site of a successful hunt?
A. The Colby site is dated at 14,000 years old.

Q. What is a Clovis point?
A. A Clovis point is a sophisticated style or method of chipping a spear or arrow point from a piece of flint or chert stone. The use of Clovis points marks a higher level of technology for stone-age man.

Q. What other mammal bones were located at the Colby Site that came from an animal that no longer exists in Wyoming today?
A. Camel bones have also been found at the site.

Q. What is the State Gem of Wyoming?
A. Jade, also known as nephrite.

Q. What purpose did ancient man first have for jade because of its toughness?
A. Early man fashioned jade into axes, knives, and projectile points before using it for ornamental and religious objects.

Q. What mineral is jade related to?
A. Asbestos.

Q. Why are the two minerals related?
A. Both jade and asbestos are composed of fibrous crystals of very similar chemical composition.

Q. Which is stronger, jade or steel?
A. Jade is stronger, being composed of fibrous, intertwining crystals.

Q. The Spanish called jade "piedra de ijada" or "loin stone." What did this signify?
A. The Spanish and South American natives believed that if the stone was worn close to the kidneys, it would heal ailments of those organs.

Q. How good is the quality of Wyoming jade?
A. Some of it is as fine a quality as any in the world.

Q. What is the largest hunk of jade found so far in Wyoming?
A. A 14,000-pound boulder was found in the southern end of the Wind River Mountains. It was of a low-quality black jade. The boulder weighed about as much as a large African elephant.

Q. What is muttonfat jade?
A. It is white jade or jade without any trace of the element iron, which gives the stone its familiar green coloration.

Q. What other green gem is often found around anthills in Wyoming?
A. Peridot is a green gem that is sometimes brought to the surface by ants as they construct their colonies in areas where it is present.

Q. What gemstone were prospectors searching for when the discovered peridot crystals around anthills?
A. They were searching for diamonds.

Q. Have any diamonds been discovered in Wyoming?
A. Yes, diamonds are actually being mined on the Wyoming/Colorado border south of Laramie.

Q. How many diamonds have been mined from this area since 1975?
A. More than 130,000.

Q. What is the percentage of gem quality stones from this mining?
A. 30 to 50 percent are gem quality

Q. What is the largest diamond recovered so far from this area?
A. It weighed more than 28 carats. This is a little more than half the size of the famous Hope Diamond, which weighs 45.5 carats. The Hope Diamond is about the diameter of a fifty cent piece, so the Wyoming stone was about the size of a quarter before it was cut and polished.

Q. What is the rare rock formation called in which diamonds are commonly found?
A. A formation of dense, blue, igneous rock from deep in the earth's crust, called a kimberlite pipe, contains the diamonds.

Q. What other precious stones are found in the kimberlite pipe formations of Wyoming?
A. High quality garnets are also found there.

Q. Wyoming has produced the largest gemstone of this type in the world. What gemstone is it?
A. Iolite, nicknamed water diamond, is a blue or violet tinted transparent stone. The record stone weighs ten and one half pounds and may be worth one million dollars in cut stones.

Q. What other precious stone has been found in significant quantities near the iolite in the Laramie Mountains?
A. Sapphires and rubies have also been found in this area.

Q. What gemstones have been found in the Red Dwarf deposit in the Granite Mountains of central Wyoming?
A. Rubies and sapphires.

Q. How big was the gold nugget that was accidentally found by a coin hunter with a metal detector in South Pass, Wyoming just a few years ago?
A. The nugget weighed 7.5 ounces and was a bit bigger than a robin's egg.

Q. Green River, Wyoming produces 90 percent of the United States' and 30 percent of the world's supply of this mineral. Name this essential mineral.
A. Green River produces a mineral called trona.

Q. What is a common name for trona and what is it used for?
A. Trona is the mineral that soda ash is derived from. It is essential to the manufacture of glass, baking soda, and many detergents.

Q. What is Green River known as?
A. Green River is known as the Trona Capital of the World.

Q. What country may surpass the United States in soda ash production by increasing its synthetic soda ash production?
A. China may surpass the United States in production.

Q. What is bentonite?
A. Bentonite is an extremely sticky clay that swells several times in size when water is added to its dried state.

Q. What is its main use?
A. Bentonite has many uses, but its primary use is to seal around the drill shafts of oil and gas wells as the drill bit pierces porous rock layers.

Q. What did pioneers and homesteaders use bentonite for?
A. They used it for hand soap and axle grease for their wagons.

Q. Where was the first bentonite processing plant in the world built?
A. Bentonite was first produced in Clay Spur, Wyoming in 1888.

Q. What state produces the most bentonite?
A. Wyoming produces over half of the bentonite used in the United States.

Q. What high energy mineral is refined into a substance called yellow cake?
A. Uranium ore is refined into a substance called yellow cake.

Q. Is any uranium mined in Wyoming?
A. Yes, Wyoming ranks first among states in uranium production.

Q. Where is the largest amount of Wyoming's uranium located?
A. The largest uranium deposits are located in an area of Fremont County known as the Gas Hills. This deposit contains at least one third of the United States' uranium reserves.

Q. What else can be found in the area of Wyoming known as Shirley Basin north of Medicine Bow, other than thousands of antelope?
A. Large deposits of uranium ore are mined in Shirley Basin.

Q. What valuable metal was discovered in the tailings dump from the Silver Cliff Mine near Lusk, Wyoming in 1919?
A. The first uranium in Wyoming was discovered in the mine tailings at Silver Cliff.

Q. In 1978, the University of Wyoming operated the largest one of these in the world on top of Jelm Mountain, Wyoming. What was it?
A. The world's largest radio telescope.

Q. Is it still the world's largest radio telescope?
A. No, it has been surpassed as the world's largest single radio telescope dish by a telescope in Arecibo, Puerto Rico, which was formed in a limestone sinkhole and covers 25 acres. Other arrays of several computer-coordinated scopes have surpassed single dishes by many times in size since 1978.

Q. What type of energy source has been tapped at Foote Creek Rim near Arlington, Wyoming?
A. A wind generating farm has been developed there because of the constant wind speeds.

Q. Why is this a good site for wind-generated electricity?
A. The wind speeds at Foote Creek average 25 miles per hour. It is one of the windiest locations in America.

Q. How much electrical power is generated at Foote Creek?
A. The wind farm is producing 85 megawatts of power, or enough electricity to power 27,000 households.

Q. Can the land that the wind turbines are located on be used for any other purpose?

A. Yes, the land is still being used for grazing livestock, just as it has been used for decades previously.

Q. What wind speeds are required for generation of electricity at Foote Creek?
A. The wind turbines will generate electricity at wind speeds between 8 and 65 miles per hour.

Q. What happens if the wind exceeds 65 miles per hour?
A. The wind turbines shut down. The turbines can with-  stand wind gusts above 125 miles per hour. They can also operate in the 30-degree-below-zero weather of Foote Ridge.

Q. How was bird life protected in the construction of the wind generators?
A. The turbines are mounted on single, tubular towers without guy wires for support, minimizing areas for birds to perch on. Power lines were buried in the ground, instead of supported on poles. The long blades spin slowly, so that birds can avoid them. The blades are even coated with a reflective ultraviolet paint that is more visible to a bird's vision. The entire site was located a short dis- tance away from the rim, where birds flew more commonly.

Q. What company built the wind generators?
A. Mitsubishi built the wind generators.

Q. What bird species is adversely affected by the wind generators?
A. Studies have shown that the noise of wind turbines has a negative effect upon sage grouse breeding grounds, otherwise known as leks.

Q. Wyoming is home to most of this species of common prairie fowl. What species is it?
A. The bulk of the sage grouse population of North America is found in Wyoming.

Q. Are there other wind farms in Wyoming?
A. Yes, there are several, including a new large facility near Evanston, Wyoming that features 80 wind turbines. This site, called the Wyoming Wind Energy Center, will produce enough energy for 48,000 homes.

Q. Where does Wyoming rank among states in the amount of wind energy that it is currently producing?
A. Wyoming is ranked ninth with 288 megawatts, just behind Oregon and ahead of Kansas.

Q. Where does Wyoming rank among the states in terms of wind generation potential?
A. Wyoming ranks seventh in wind generation potential.

Q. What state ranks first in wind energy potential?
A. North Dakota ranks first.

Q. What is coal gasification?
A. Coal gasification is the process of extracting energy from coal by squeezing the gases out of it under high pressure and burning them to create electric energy, instead of burning the whole coal. This process is cleaner than burning whole coal.

Q. Does coal gasification work with Wyoming coal?
A. No, gasification does not work very well with Wyoming coals at this time because they are often too moist and not developed completely yet because the coal beds were not buried as deeply nor for as long as other coal beds in the U.S.

Q. Is there interest in developing processes to use Wyoming coal for gasification?
A. Yes; because Wyoming produces nearly 40 percent of the United States' coal, several companies, such as GE Coal Gasification, are researching methods to adapt their gasification processes to Wyoming coal.

Q. What did a rancher notice seeping from a fence post hole near Byron, Wyoming?
A. The rancher spotted natural gas escaping from the vacated fence post hole. The fumes were lighted and they burned for several years. The area was soon drilled successfully for natural gas.

Q. What is the Wyoming State Dinosaur, whose name means three-horned face?
A. The Triceratops.

Q. This Triceratops body-part was larger than the same part of any land animal that has ever roamed the Earth. Name it.
A. The Triceratops had the largest head, which was over ten feet long.

Q. How long was a Triceratops?
A. They reached lengths of thirty feet.

Q. Were Triceratops very smart?
A. No one knows for sure, but they had relatively large brain capacities and eye sockets, which generally indicates expanded intelligence.

Q. Who chose the Triceratops as Wyoming's State Dinosaur?
A. Wyoming schoolchildren made the choice on March 18, 1994.

Q. What was the first fossil of a Triceratops mistaken for?
A. It was mistaken for an extinct species of bison.

Q. Were there many Triceratops in Wyoming?
A. Yes, they once roamed in large herds during the Cretaceous Period, perhaps much as the bison did in the 19th Century.

Q. What probably ended the days of the Triceratops?
A. Some scientists theorize a large meteor struck the earth in what is now the Gulf of Mexico. This disaster caused a worldwide climatic change, which exterminated the Triceratops, as well as many other life forms on the planet.

Q. What is unique about one of the Triceratops fossils being excavated in Wyoming?
A. An example of its skin texture is present.

Q. What other state has the Triceratops as its state fossil?
A. South Dakota.

Q. What was unique about the Billed Dinosaur found in Niobrara County, Wyoming?
A. A fossilized Billed Dinosaur was found with its skin still completely intact. The fossilized skin texture gave scientists a rare look at the relatively small size of scales covering this 15-foot-tall, 30-foot-long dinosaur.

Q. Why does the Sinclair Oil Company use a dinosaur as its symbol?
A. During oil exploration near Greybull, Wyoming in the late 1920s, Sinclair Oil discovered a large bed of dinosaur fossils. The area contained over twenty complete dinosaur skeletons.

Q. What dinosaur does the Sinclair Oil Company use as its symbol?
A. The Apatosaur, formerly called Brontosaurus.

Q. Where can a person help excavate dinosaurs at a real dinosaur dig?
A. The general public may participate in actual dinosaur digs during the Dig-For-A-Day program at the Wyoming Dinosaur Center, located in Thermopolis, Wyoming.

Q. What is unique about the stone house of Jody Fultz at Como Bluff, Wyoming?
A. The stones of the house, as well as an accompanying museum, are dinosaur bones from the extensive fossil quarry nearby.

Q. How many dinosaur bones compose the Como Bluff house?
A. The house contains 5,796 dinosaur bones, all more than two million years old.

Q. What is the name given to the brilliant red rock outcroppings and walls seen in many locations in Wyoming?
A. The red rock formations are called the Chugwater formations, and denote a certain geologic time range for the surface area around them.

Q. How old is the Chugwater Formation?
A. It occurred during the Triassic Age, or 210 million years ago. The earliest dinosaurs appeared in the middle portion of this age; and the earliest mammals at its end.

Q. What is the Wyoming State Reptile?
A. The horned toad, or *Douglassi brevirostre*, is the Wyoming state reptile.

Q. How many other states use the horned toad as their state reptile?
A. Only one other state—Texas.

Q. Is the horned toad really a toad?
A. No, it is a lizard and its "horns" are really enlarged scales.

Q. What does the horned toad symbolize for some Native American tribes?
A. It symbolizes strength.

Q. How does the horned toad survive in winter?
A. It hibernates.

Q. How does the horned toad drink water?
A. It channels rain water down its short, stubby tail, along its back, and into its mouth.

Q. What is a horned toad's favorite food?
A. It prefers ants most of all.

Q. How many eggs does a mother horned toad lay in one clutch?
A. She may lay as many as 30 eggs, which are buried in the earth and hatch five to nine weeks later.

Q. What unique defense does a horned toad use to discourage predators from eating it?
A. A horned toad can squirt blood, laced with a toxic, nasty-tasting substance, from its eyes when it is threatened.

Q. How far can the horned toad squirt this blood?
A. The horned toad is actually listed in *Ripley's Believe It or Not* as being able to squirt blood a distance of five feet.

Q. Where was the first land set aside as a sanctuary for wild horses?
A. The Pryor Mountain Wild Horse Range, north of Lovell, Wyoming was the first refuge set aside for wild horses by the United States government in 1968.

Q. Where did the Pryor Mountains get their name?
A. The mountains were named for Sergeant Nathaniel Pryor of the Lewis and Clark Expedition. Clark sent Pryor and some other men after some horses stolen by the Crow Indians of the region. Sergeant Pryor did not recover the horses.

Q. How many wild horses live on the Pryor Mountain Wild Horse Range?
A. Approximately 120 wild horses live on the Pryor Mountain Wild Horse Range.

Q. Can the wild horses be viewed on their reserve?
A. Yes, primitive roads do exist and may be traveled by four-wheel-drive vehicles. The Bighorn Canyon National Recreation Area also borders the Wild Horse Refuge, and the horses may be seen along a stretch of a paved highway that runs through it.

Q. Where did wild horses come from?
A. American wild horses, or mustangs, descended mostly from horses that escaped or were taken from early Spanish ranches of the Southwest. It has been genetically proven that the Pryor Mountain herds are true descendents of these Spanish mustangs.

Q. What unusual feature is sometimes seen upon the legs of Pryor Mountain mustangs that is a legacy of their relations in Africa?
A. Some Pryor Mountain mustangs have faint striping on their legs, somewhat like the coats of zebras in Africa.

Q. Are Pryor Mountain mustangs large horses?
A. No, as with most wild horses, they are somewhat small—averaging 15 hands high or five feet high at the shoulder. Smaller stature helps them to conserve energy in their harsh environment. Thoroughbred horses, the type of horse used in racing and once used by the military, are generally over 16 hands in height, and of a more slender, leggier build.

Q. Can a person acquire a Pryor Mountain mustang?
A. Yes, about 50 of the horses are put up for adoption once every year to maintain the size of the herd on the limited grazing of the refuge.

Q. What other measures are being used to control the population of the herds?
A. One- and two-year-old mares are given long-term birth control injections at each autumn round-up.

Q. How many wild horses existed in the United States at the beginning of the 20th Century?

A. Over 300,000 wild horses roamed the western states.

Q. How many wild horses roam free in the United States today?
A. About 37,000 wild horses roam free in the United States today.

Q. In the 1920's, cattlemen decided that the wild horses were competing with their cattle and should be destroyed. A bounty was placed upon wild horses. How much was the bounty?
A. Four dollars was paid for the destruction of each wild horse.

Q. How did the bounty hunter prove the number of horses that he had killed?
A. He brought the tip of each horse's ear into the government agencies.

Q. Where does Wyoming rank as a state in the number of wild horses that it contains?
A. Wyoming has the second largest number of wild horses of any state.

Q. What state has a larger wild horse herd?
A. Nevada has a larger herd.

Q. What ocean does the water drain to, from Union Pass, west of Dubois, Wyoming?
A. Three streams actually drain the pass. One eventually flows to the Columbia River and the Pacific Ocean. Another drains to the east and the Mississippi River and the Gulf of Mexico. The third stream drains into the Colorado River drainage and the Sea of Cortez.

Q. How large is the Red Desert of south-central Wyoming?
A. The Red Desert contains over 700 square miles, or about half the size of Rhode Island.

Q. What river drains the Red Desert of southwestern Wyoming?
A. No river drains it. The Great Divide splits around either side of the Great Divide Basin, which contains the Red Desert, and does not allow drainage to the Pacific or the Atlantic. Moisture evaporates rapidly enough so that no permanent streams exiting the basin are formed.

Q. Name the two largest ancient volcanic plugs in Wyoming.
A. Devil's Tower would be the largest. The Boar's Tusk, found in the Red Desert, is the second largest.

Q. What mammal forms the herds that create the longest migration in the continental United States?
A. Antelope migrate hundreds of miles from the Red Desert to Grand Teton National Park in large herds.

Q. What large western mammal is found in the Red Desert that you would not expect to find there?
A. A rare herd of desert-dwelling elk inhabit the Red Desert.

Q. What should you be careful to watch out for near rock outcrops in the southwestern part of the Red Desert?
A. A tiny rattlesnake, called the midget faded rattlesnake, lives there. This snake's venom is actually more toxic than that of its larger cousin, the diamondback, in spite of its diminutive size.

Q. What landform do scientists refer to as a "ghoroud" or an "erg"?
A. Sand fields may be called "ghorouds" or "ergs." "Ghoroud" is the ancient Egyptian word for a sand field, while "erg" is the Arabic form.

Q. The second-largest example of this mobile land form in the world is found in the Red Desert. Name it.
A. The Killpecker Sand Dunes of the Red Desert are the second-largest example of moving, active sand dunes in the world. They are nearly 50 miles long and ten miles wide in places.

Q. Where is the largest area of moving sand dunes in the world?
A. An area in the Great Nefud Desert of Saudi Arabia, called Jafura, covers an area of 550 square miles with moving sand dunes. This dune field stretches over 100 miles in length and is five miles wide.

Q. What is the name for the branch of geography that involves the study of moving sand?
A. This field is known as Eolian geography—named for Aeolus, the Greek god of winds.

Q. If geologists were classifying something using the terms crescent, linear, star, parabolic, whale back, and dome-shaped, what would they be discussing?
A. They would be using official classifications of sand dunes.

Q. What factors are necessary for a sand dune to form?
A. Wind, sand, and an object to interrupt the flow of the wind and allow the sand to pile up behind it are required to form a sand dune.

Q. What happens to the object that causes the formation of the dune?
A. It is buried.

Q. What unique sound might be heard in a dune field?
A. The rare phenomenon of "dune song" may be heard. A squeaking or a low humming can be produced by sand dunes on rare occasions. This sound is thought to originate from internal friction within the dunes.

Q. Where did the name Killpecker come from?
A. Pioneers drank the alkaline water found in springs nearby and noticed a temporary decline in their sex lives.

Q. If the Killpecker Dunes are part of a desert, what causes mysterious pools of water to form there from time to time?
A. Ancient ice is trapped inside the dunes and, as the dunes roll along, the ice becomes exposed and melts to form the pools.

Q. What type of animal exists in higher con-centrations in the Red Desert than anywhere in the country?
A. The Red Desert has a larger concentration of raptors (hawks, eagles, falcons, and vultures) than any other place in the United States.

Q. Where was the last wild bison herd exterminated in Wyoming?
A. The last wild bison in Wyoming was killed in the Red Desert in the 1890s. A few bison remained in Yellowstone Park, but they were not considered free-roaming.

Q. What is the greatest threat to the Red Desert today?
A. Oil and natural gas exploration and development of the area could destroy the fragile ecosystem.

Q. How did Saratoga, Wyoming get its name?
A. The town was named after the health resort town of Saratoga Springs in the state of New York. Saratoga, Wyoming also has hot springs utilized for health purposes. The hot springs water here is 114 degrees Fahrenheit, clear, and odorless.

Q. What modern-day, enlightening invention had its beginnings on the shores of Battle Lake, near Encampment, Wyoming?
A. While gazing at bamboo shards from his broken fishing rod in 1878, Thomas Edison conceived the idea of an electrically charged carbon filament to create light, thus the beginnings of the light bulb.

Q. Why was Thomas Edison in Wyoming?
A. Edison was there as part of an expedition headed by astronomer Henry Draper to observe the 1878 solar eclipse.

Q. What was the first city in the world to receive electric incandescent lighting?
A. Cheyenne, Wyoming was the first city in the world to be lighted by electricity.

Q. When was this lighting system installed?
A. The lights were installed in 1882.

Q. Who installed the lighting?
A. The fledgling electric company of Bush-Swan Electric Light Company had opened business in Cheyenne and provided battery-powered lighting throughout the city. The batteries were recharged during daylight hours by a steam- driven dynamo or generator.

Q. What is the "Big Boy" that can be seen in Holiday Park in Cheyenne, Wyoming?
A. Big Boy is the nickname for the world's largest steam locomotive, officially named Number 4004.

Q. How many Big Boys were built?
A. Twenty-five Big Boy locomotives were built.

Q. When were they built and used?
A. The first Big Boys were built in 1941. The huge steam locomotives were retired in 1962.

Q. Why is Number 4004 in Cheyenne?
A. The engine is retired now, but it was built to haul trains over the mountains from Cheyenne to Ogden, Utah. It has been replaced by modern diesel-electric locomotives.

Q. How large is the Big Boy?
A. The Big Boy is nearly 133 feet long, or nearly half a football field in length. It weighs 1,208,000 pounds or 604 tons. Its four pistons are two feet in diameter and nearly three feet long. Sixteen drive wheels, set in two groups of eight—four on a side for each group—are over five feet high. The engine is so long that it has to bend in the middle, or articulate, to turn corners. It has four smaller steering wheels at each end, two on a side for each group.

Q. How many elementary-age school children were packed into the firebox of one Big Boy locomotive to demonstrate its size?
A. 32 children were able to squeeze into the space where coal was burned to fire the boiler and provide steam for a Big Boy locomotive.

Q. How powerful is the Big Boy?
A. It is twice as powerful as a regular steam locomotive of its era.

Q. How fast was Big Boy?
A. Big Boy could run at speeds up to 80 miles per hour. It ran efficiently at 60 to 70 miles per hour, which was unusual for such a powerful locomotive.

Q. How much water did old Number 4004 carry for its boilers?
A. Number 4004 carried 25,000 gallons of water.

Q. How much coal was on board to fuel the trip?
A. 28 tons of coal were on board.

Q. What was an essential characteristic about the Big Boy locomotives during the 1940s?
A. The Big Boy locomotives were easy to operate, even by inexperienced crew. These locomotives were operated during World War II, when large numbers of trained railroad personnel had gone into the Armed Forces. These people were replaced by inexperienced men who were unfit for military service.

Q. Is Number 4004 in running condition today?
A. No, none of the Big Boy locomotives still in existence is in running condition.

Q. What is the largest steam locomotive that is in running condition today?
A. The Union Pacific Challenger Number 3985 has been restored to running condition. It is only slightly smaller than Number 4004. Challenger does not run on a regular schedule, but makes an occasional excursion run for publicity.

Q. Where is Number 3985 located?
A. It is also located in Cheyenne, Wyoming.

Q. Are there pyramids in Wyoming?
A. There is one for certain. It is the Ames pyramid, a monument honoring Oliver and Oakes Ames. It is located eighteen miles east of Laramie, Wyoming.

Q. How tall is the Ames Pyramid?
A. It is sixty feet tall and made of granite.

Q. Why is it located in the middle of nowhere?
A. The brothers Ames were promoters of the Transcontinental Railroad. A town called Sherman once existed at the location of the pyramid. Trains stopped here for

inspection after climbing a steep grade and before descending another long, steep grade. The tracks were relocated at a later date and the town gradually disappeared.

Q. Does Wyoming have a Lincoln Memorial?
A. Yes, there is a 12' 6" bronze bust of Abraham Lincoln mounted on top of a thirty-foot granite column, standing on top of 8,640-foot Sherman Hill, thirty miles west of Cheyenne.

Q. Why is Lincoln's monument located here?
A. This is the highest point of the first transcontinental railroad. The transcontinental railroad was one of Lincoln's ambitions for the country.

Q. What is the name of the highway that passes by this Lincoln monument?
A. The highway is U.S. 30, or the Lincoln Highway.

Q. What was the first automobile purchased and brought to Wyoming?
A. Elmer Lovejoy of Laramie bought a Locomobile steam-powered automobile in 1899. Gasoline or kerosene was used to heat the water into steam in the boiler of the automobile.

Q. How big was a Locomobile?
A. A 1899 Locomobile was 4 feet 5 inches wide by 7 feet three inches long, weighing 700 pounds. The cab was 5 feet 4 inches tall and it rode on four 28-inch-diameter bicycle wheels. Two people could ride in the overgrown-baby-buggy-looking car.

Q. Was this Elmer's first automobile?
A. No, he built one for himself in his shop in 1897. It weighed 940 pounds.

Q. What little-known natural wonder is found 28 miles south of Douglas, Wyoming?
A. Ayres Natural Bridge, a natural rock arch with a top height of 50 feet and a span of 150 feet, is located there.

Q. How large is Ayres Natural Bridge?
A. The natural arch is fifty feet wide and thirty feet from the ground at the center of its arch.

Q. Ayres Natural Bridge is one of only three natural arches in the world to still have this unusual condition. What is the condition?
A. The stream that formed it still runs beneath it. In this case, LaPrele Creek passes beneath the arch.

Q. How long is the Tongue River Cave system in the Tongue River Canyon?
A. The Tongue River Cave system is over 2.5 miles long.

Q. Is the Tongue River Cave system developed for use by tourists?
A. No, the cave system is in its natural state and should only be explored with an experienced guide or spelunker.

Q. What is unique about the Lower Kane cave system near the Bighorn River in Wyoming?
A. This cave system was formed by sulfuric acid dissolving the rock, instead of water. Microbes in the soil and the water of the cave are producing the sulfuric acid that is, in turn, carving out the cave.

Q. What cave system is the longest in Wyoming?
A. The Horse Thief cave system is over ten miles long and is the largest in Wyoming.

Q. What is the deepest cave in Wyoming?
A. At 1,551 feet deep, the Columbine Crawl is the deepest cave in Wyoming, and the third deepest cave in the continental United States. The cave is located in the Teton Mountains.

Q. Which cave has the largest room in Wyoming?
A. The Great Expectations Cave in the Bighorn Mountains has the largest room. The space is nearly one half mile long, 100 feet tall, and 100 feet wide in places.

Q. If Jewel Cave had another entrance in Wyoming, other than its only entrance just across the state line in South Dakota—even though a good portion of the cave system lies below the surface of Wyoming—what rank could Wyoming claim in containing the world's longest caves?
A. Wyoming would rank second in the world, along with South Dakota. Jewel Cave is over 135 miles long and still being explored.

HISTORY

Q. Sacagawea was the Shoshone Indian woman who traveled with Lewis and Clark on part of their expedition to explore the Louisiana Purchase. Where is Sacagawea buried?
A. A plot that is claimed to be her gravesite, along with those of two of her sons, is located at Fort Washakie, a small town on the Wind River Indian Reservation in central Wyoming.

Q. The headstone at Fort Washakie suggests that Sacagawea was how old when she died?
A. The grave is dated April 9, 1884, which would have made Sacagawea about 96 years old at her death.

Q. Where else is Sacagawea supposed to be buried?
A. Another gravesite is located on the Standing Rock Sioux Indian Reservation near Mobridge, South Dakota. It is on the location of old Fort Manuel Lisa.

Q. How old was Sacagawea when she died at the site in South Dakota?
A. She died, according to historical record, on December 20, 1812, of a fever, at the age of 25.

Q. What great leader of the Shoshone tribe was buried with full military honors in 1900 and given the rank of captain?
A. Chief Washakie, who is buried near Sacagawea in the Chief Washakie Cemetery on the Wind River Indian Reservation.

Q. What structure served as the first jail in Cheyenne, Wyoming?
A. A tent served as the jail in Cheyenne, in 1868.

Q. In 1883, a printer in Cheyenne, Wyoming ran out of white paper and decided to substitute yellow paper for the item that he was printing. What did this item become the first example of?
A. He was printing a telephone directory. He created the first Yellow Pages.

Q. What did two deviously creative people from Kentucky do in the Red Desert of Wyoming in 1872 to reap a large profit on a $35,000 investment?
A. The two con men, Arnold and Slack, sprinkled $35,000 worth of uncut gems across the Red Desert, then sold the rights to mine the area to a San Francisco bank for $600,000.

Q. How was the hoax discovered?
A. A German miner, local to the Green River, Wyoming area, searched for and found the gem-salted area and discovered that many of the gems had already been partially cut and polished.

Q. Were Arnold and Slack ever brought to justice for their scam?
A. Slack was never found. Arnold was a native of Kentucky and his home state would not extradite him to California. He eventually agreed to pay $150,000 back to the bank in California to escape further prosecution. He was shot dead in a personal conflict one year after making that settlement.

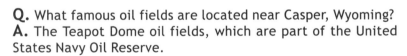

Q. When was the first oil well drilled in Wyoming?
A. It was drilled in 1884.

Q. Where was this first well drilled?
A. It was drilled nine miles south of Lander, Wyoming.

Q. What famous oil fields are located near Casper, Wyoming?
A. The Teapot Dome oil fields, which are part of the United States Navy Oil Reserve.

Q. Why are these oil fields called Teapot Dome?
A. The area is named after an unusual rock formation that resembles a huge teapot.

Q. Who shot and killed Billy the Kid in a darkened room in the middle of the night in New Mexico?
A. Pat Garrett.

Q. Who shot Pat Garrett in the back and and killed when he stopped his wagon and stepped off to relieve himself during an argument?
A. Wayne Brazel shot Garrett near Las Cruces, New Mexico.

Q. Who successfully defended Wayne Brazel on the murder of Pat Garrett, pleading self-defense?
A. Albert Fall., who often defended cattle rustlers in the area.

Q. Who did President Warren Harding appoint as Secretary of the Interior in 1921?
A. Albert Fall.

Q. What is Albert Fall most famous for?
A. In 1922, Albert Fall was convicted of accepting bribes from two oil companies to lease the Teapot Dome oil fields near Casper, Wyoming without any competitive bidding.

Q. What amount was Albert Fall "loaned," without interest, from Edward Doherty of the Pan American Petroleum and Transport Company, in exchange for the unchallenged right to lease the Teapot Dome oil field from the U. S. Navy Oil Reserves?
A. $100,000.

Q. What was Albert Fall's sentence for accepting the bribes?
A. He was forced to resign, he was sentenced to one year in prison, and he was fined $100,000.

Q. Who else was forced to resign his government position because of the scandal?
A. Edwin Denby, Secretary of the Navy, was also forced to resign because of his involvement.

Q. Did President Harding know about the illegal arrangements of Albert Fall and Edwin Denby?
A. Yes, President Harding acknowledged that he had okayed the dealings with Edward Doherty and Harry F. Sinclair, owner of Mammoth Oil Corporation.

Q. What punishment did President Warren Harding receive?
A. President Harding died in office before any judicial action took place., and was replaced by Calvin Coolidge.

Q. Did either oil company owner receive any sentence in the scandal?
A. Yes, Harry Sinclair had hired private detectives to shadow and intimidate jury members during the trial. He was sentenced to six months in prison on related charges.

Q. What did the town of Parco, Wyoming change its name to in 1934?
A. Parco became Sinclair in honor of Harry Sinclair.

Q. How many years has Teapot Dome produced oil?
A. The Teapot Dome Oilfield is over one hundred years old

Q. What new process is being tested at the Teapot Dome fields that will improve oil production in older fields or in oil fields where oil is difficult to recover?
A. Carbon dioxide is being injected into the rock formations for storage and to attempt to increase pressure upon the oil to force it from the rock.

Q. How much might carbon dioxide injection increase the production of oil in the Teapot Dome oil field?
A. It may increase the oil production from 5,300 barrels a day to nearly 35,000 barrels a day, or more than a six-fold increase.

Q. What is important about being able to store carbon dioxide in rock formations?
A. Carbon dioxide is a greenhouse gas produced in large quantities by coal-burning electric generation plants. Storing it underground will prevent its harming the atmosphere.

Q. Where will the carbon dioxide (CO_2) originate from to inject into the Teapot Dome field?
A. A 125-mile-long pipeline is being built from the Shute Creek natural-gas processing plant in western Wyoming to the oil field. The CO_2 is a by-product of the natural gas processing operation.

Q. Who pays for this pipeline?
A. Anadarko Petroleum Company will pay up to two-thirds of the cost, while the U.S. government will fund about one-third.

Q. How long will this project last?
A. Seven to ten years.

Q. What major department store chain was started in the small Wyoming town of Kemmerer?
A. The J. C. Penney Store began its existence in 1902.

Q. The 'J' in J. C. Penney stood for James. What did the middle initial 'C' stand for?
A. It stood for his middle name, "Cash."

Q. What was J. C. Penney's father's occupation?
A. He was a Baptist minister

Q. What was the name of James Cash Penney's first store?
A. It was called The Golden Rule Store, signifying that Mr. Penney would treat his costumers as he would wish them to treat him.

Q. Was J. C. Penney the originator of the name, Golden Rule Store?
A. No, he bought a partnership in the Golden Rule Store Franchise that belonged to two men whom he had been working for, Guy Johnson and Thomas Callahan. Over time, these two men tired of the business and sold it all to Penney.

Q. Where did J. C. Penney house his family when he opened his first store in Kemmerer?
A. The Penneys lived in the attic over the one-room store.

Q. What business practice did J. C. Penney initiate that was unusual for his day?
A. He charged everyone the same price for any particular item. Other merchants would charge a customer a price of their choosing, according to socio-economic status of the customer.

Q. Were J. C. Penney credit cards available when James Cash Penney started his business?
A. Certainly not! In fact, J. C. Penney did not believe in issuing

credit in any form to his customers and that was a rare business practice in western ranch communities.

Q. What were customers sometimes surprised to find occurring in any one of J. C. Penney's hundreds of department stores?
A. A customer might find Penney himself wrapping packages, waiting on customers, or even sweeping the floor if he happened to be visiting the store.

Q. At what age did J. C. Penney die?
A. James Cash Penney lived 95 years.

Q. What famous law was first enacted in Green River, Wyoming and has since been adopted by thousands of other communities throughout the United States?
A. The Green River Ordinance, created in 1931, made door-to-door sales illegal in the town of Green River.

Q. Why didn't the city of Green River want door-to-door salesmen pounding on the doors of its inhabitants during the day?
A. Most of the men of Green River were miners and many worked at night. The town wished to prevent any disruption to their daytime sleep.

Q. Why does George Lathrop have a monument dedicated to him located two miles west of Lusk, Wyoming on Highway 20?
A. George Lathrop was the last stagecoach driver to take a stage over the Cheyenne-Deadwood stage route. The marker is located at George Lathrop's gravesite. Friends requested that the monument be erected to honor this popular driver.

Q. What was George Lathrop's prized possession and a symbol of his trade?
A. His 20-foot-long whip with the first two feet of handle encased in silver ferrules.

Q. During what years was the Cheyenne-Deadwood Stage active?
A. The stagecoaches traveled between Cheyenne and Deadwood, South Dakota daily from 1876 to 1887.

Q. How long did a trip from Cheyenne to Deadwood take on the stage coach?
A. The stage traveled 300 miles in 50 hours if all went well.

Q. How often did the stage change horses?
A. The stage changed teams every fifteen miles.

Q. How much did a ticket cost to ride the stage?
A. Five dollars got a traveler a seat on top by the driver. Ten dollars landed a seat inside the middle of the coach. Fifteen bought a window seat.

Q. Where were the stagecoaches built that were used on the Cheyenne-to-Deadwood Stage route?
A. The Concord coaches were built in Concord, New Hampshire.

Q. How did the coaches arrive in Cheyenne?
A. The coaches traveled by ship around Cape Horn at the southern extremity of South America to the California coast. They were then shipped by railroad to Cheyenne.

Q. What absorbed some of the shocks and jolts of the bumpy road to and from Deadwood?
A. The cabins of the Concord coaches were hung on large leather straps, hammock style. These strips were called thoroughbraces.

Q. What might you stumble into if you drive your golf ball far into the rough on the Guernsey, Wyoming golf course?
A. Ruts of the Oregon Trail are ground deeply into the sandstone near the Guernsey golf course.

Q. "Galvanized Yankees" were used to explore parts of southeast Wyoming. What were "Galvanized Yankees?"
A. They were Confederate prisoners of war who volunteered to serve in the Union army on the western frontier.

Q. Could a steamboat have entered Wyoming?
A. Yes, the steamboat *El Paso* actually penetrated the boundaries of present-day Wyoming in 1851 when it ascended the North Platte River to the location of modern-day Guernsey. The river was deemed too shallow for commercial use.

Q. Where does the North Platte River get its name?
A. "Platte" is the French word for "flat." The Platte River is often described as a mile wide and an inch deep.

Q. What domestic function was made easy at a place near Guernsey for travelers on the Oregon Trail?
A. Pioneers could do their laundry at the Emigrant's Wash Tub at any time of year because the water in this pool stays warm naturally in any season of the year due to geothermal activity beneath it.

Q. What Old West mountain man did Robert Redford portray in 1972?
A. Jeremiah Johnson (sometimes spelled Johnston).

Q. Where is Jeremiah "Liver-eating" Johnson buried?
A. He is buried in Old Trail Town, a museum and collection of historic buildings in Cody, Wyoming.

Q. Has he always been buried there?
A. No, he was moved from the Veterans Cemetery in Los Angeles, California, and reburied in Cody in 1974 by Bob Edgar, the creator of Old Trail Town.

Q. Why was he buried in a veterans cemetery in Los Angeles?
A. He died in Los Angeles on January 22, 1900. He had been a soldier in the Civil War.

Q. Who attended the reburial?
A. Robert Redford, along with over 2,000 other people.

Q. Was Jeremiah his actual name?
A. No, his first name was John.

Q. Did John Johnson actually eat human livers?
A. Yes, he ate the livers of Crow warriors. He killed these warriors in revenge for their murdering his Indian wife and unborn child.

Q. Where can you stand in an actual building that Butch Cassidy and the Sundance Kid spent time in?
A. Old Trail Town has several buildings where Butch and Sundance, and other famous western outlaws, passed the time. These buildings were collected and moved here from locations throughout Wyoming by Old Trail Town's founder, Bob Edgar.

Q. What was the original purpose for the land that Old Trail Town stands on?
A. Buffalo Bill Cody and his surveyors had laid out the plan for the original town of Cody City on the site.

Q. What brought many Germans and Italians to the Douglas, Wyoming area in 1943?
A. German and Italian prisoners of war were brought to a newly constructed POW camp near Douglas in 1943.

Q. What annual event determined when the POWs were allowed to return to Europe after World War II ended in 1945?
A. The German and Italian soldiers had worked on local farms and in local lumber camps. They were allowed to return to their homelands after the harvest in 1945.

Q. What grim episode in American history occurred in the shadow of Heart Mountain, located half way between Cody and Powell, Wyoming?
A. Eleven thousand Japanese were relocated from their homes across the United States to an internment camp at the base of Heart Mountain during World War II.

Q. Were these people spies or, at least, foreigners?
A. No, most of these people were born in the United States, and so were citizens.

Q. Where did the Heart Mountain Relocation Center rate in terms of community size in Wyoming in 1945?
A. It was the third largest city in Wyoming at that time, with a population of 10,767 people at its peak.

Q. If so many Japanese-Americans were relocated to ten different camps across the U.S., did any Japanese-Americans serve in the Armed Forces during World War II?
A. The United States government sent over 700 men their draft notices at Heart Mountain Camp alone. 385 of these men were drafted into the armed services. Eleven of these Japanese soldiers lost their lives in battle; 52 were wounded.

Q. What famous unit in the Army did the Japanese-American soldiers serve in?
A. Most Japanese-American soldiers served in the 442nd Regimental Combat Team. The 442nd served in Europe and North Africa. It was the most decorated unit in the history of the U.S. Army.

Q. What happened to a Japanese-American who refused to be drafted?
A. These men were sent to prison. Eighty-five men from Heart Mountain refused to be drafted. Three hundred and fifteen men refused from all ten internment camps.

Q. What happened to the relocated Japanese' homes and businesses?
A. Much of their personal property was lost to other American citizens during their internment.

Q. How many buildings made up the Heart Mountain Relocation Camp?
A. 468 buildings were constructed to house the internees.

Q. What were the buildings constructed of?
A. The large, barracks-style buildings were plank-walled buildings covered with tar paper. Each building was divided up to house single people, couples, and families. Rooms contained a stove, a ceiling light, cots, and two blankets per person.

Q. How long did the construction of the camp take?
A. The camp was ready for the first occupants in sixty days.

Q. What kept the internees from leaving the camp?
A. The compound was surrounded by barbed wire. Soldiers manned nine guard towers. Powerful search lights scanned the camp at night.

Q. What did the internees do to occupy their time?
A. They dug 5,000-foot-long canal for irrigation. They raised crops and livestock. They made clothing and furniture. They produced lumber at a sawmill and printed posters and a newspaper at a printing shop. They worked as farm laborers on local farms when they were allowed.

Q. Were these people paid for this employment?
A. Yes, but none of them could be paid more than an army private made—$21 per month.

Q. Was the patriotism of the Japanese-Americans ever evaluated in the camp?
A. Yes, a "loyalty questionnaire" was administered to the internees. 95.5 percent of them passed. Having passed the test, they were eligible to leave to other designated locations and activities in the United States, after a great deal of paper work.

Q. When World War II ended and the internees were allowed to leave, how were they compensated?
A. Each internee was given $25.00 and a train ticket home, if their homes had not been confiscated by others.

Q. How much remains of the Heart Mountain Relocation Camp today?
A. Only a few buildings and the smoke stack from the hospital furnace room remain.

Q. What was called "The Great Register in the Desert" by Father Pierre De Smet in 1841?
A. Located about sixty miles southwest of Casper, it is Independence Rock, which is engraved with the names of more than 5,000 pioneers on the Oregon Trail.

Q. Why is this landmark called Independence Rock?
A. Originally, fur trappers held a rendezvous celebration at this spot on July 4th, Independence Day, in 1830. Later, wagon trains hoped to have reached this spot on or before July 4th to know that they were on schedule to be in the Oregon Territory before winter.

Q. How tall is Independence Rock?
A. It is 193 feet tall.

Q. Where was Wyoming's first Masonic Lodge meeting held?
A. It was held on top of Independence Rock on July 4, 1862 —
Independence Day.

Q. What other name was the woman of ill repute Ella Watson
known by?
A. She was known as Cattle Kate.

Q. Was this because of her unusual size?
A. No, she was called Cattle Kate because she sometimes took
stolen cattle as payment for her services.

Q. What was known as a "hog ranch" in Wyoming?
A. A house of ill repute was often referred to as a hog ranch,
especially if its girls were very unattractive or nearing the ends
of their careers.

Q. What happened to Cattle Kate and her boyfriend, James Averell?
A. The two were hanged by a lynch mob of six or more men
because they were believed to be accepting stolen cattle. The
vigilantes admitted to the crime of taking the law into their
own hands.

Q. Was there really much evidence of cattle rustling by Cattle
Kate and her partner at the time of their hanging?
A. No stolen cattle were evident, nor was any other proof of
crime available.

Q. Were any of the lynching party ever brought to justice?
A. No, all participants were arrested, but released on five thousand dollar bonds. None of the men was ever brought to trial.

Q. Where was Cattle Kate's ranch located?
A. It was located about three miles from Independence Rock.

Q. Was any other woman ever hanged in Wyoming?
A. No other woman has ever been hanged in Wyoming legally and
no records exist of a woman being lynched, except for Cattle Kate.

Q. Was a woman ever convicted of cattle rustling in Wyoming?
A. Yes, Ann Richey was convicted in 1919 and sentenced to six years in prison. She never served her sentence. She was poisoned by an unknown person while she was free on bond.

Q. What did the citizens of Rawlins, Wyoming do with the mortal remains of George "Big Nose" Parrot after they lynched him in March of 1881?
A. They skinned him, tanned his hide, and made garments of the leather. Several known outlaws left town when the clothing went on display.

Q. Why did the citizens of Rawlins lynch George Parrot?
A. He tried unsuccessfully to rob a train and, when pursued, killed two lawmen before he was apprehended. He then beat up a guard in a prison escape attempt.

Q. What famous outlaw reportedly accompanied Parrot on the train robbery attempt?
A. Frank James, Jesse James' brother, was rumored to be an accomplice.

Q. Dr. John Osborne was the actual skinner of "Big Nose" George. Did Dr. Osborne rise to any higher station in life than a simple country doctor and boot maker?
A. Yes, he was elected as Wyoming governor in 1892 and became a United States Congressman in 1897. He wore a pair of "Big Nose" Parrot shoes to his inaugural ball as Wyoming governor.

Q. Is any of this macabre clothing still in existence?
A. Yes, a pair of shoes and the top of George's skull are on display at Rawlins National Bank Museum at 220 Fifth Street in Rawlins.

Q. Why is the skull cap still in existence?
A. It was used as a doorstop by Wyoming's first female doctor, Lillian Nelson, for many years.

Q. What United States vice president claims Wyoming as his home state?
A. Vice president Richard Cheney.

Q. Who killed "Wild Bill" Hickok in a gambling house in Deadwood, South Dakota?
A. Jack "Broken Nose" McCall.

Q. Where was McCall arrested for the murder?
A. He was arrested in Laramie, Wyoming, 28 days after the murder, and returned to South Dakota for a second trial.

Q. Was this the first arrest for Hickok's murder?
A. No, McCall had been arrested on the spot in Deadwood, but had been acquitted in a speedy trial because he claimed that he shot Hickok in revenge for Hickok's killing of his brother.

Q. Why was McCall tried again?
A. The first trial was held in Deadwood, which was on an Indian reservation and had no recognized court system. The second trial was held at the South Dakota territorial capitol in Yankton.

Q. What was the outcome of the new trial?
A. It was discovered that McCall did not have any brothers, only sisters, so he was found guilty and hanged in 1877.

Q. What final token of disdain was discovered when McCall's coffin was moved to a new location several years later?
A. The coffin was opened and "Broken Nose's" corpse still had the hangman's noose encircling his neck.

Q. What famous outlaw gang seized control of Baggs, Wyoming after robbing a bank in Nevada of $35,000?
A. Butch Cassidy and the Wild Bunch stopped in Baggs for a little rest and relaxation and to spend some of their hard-earned loot from Nevada.

Q. Where is the famous hideout of Butch Cassidy and the Sundance Kid, known as the Hole in the Wall, located?
A. The Hole in the Wall is located about thirty miles west of Kaycee, Wyoming.

Q. What was Butch Cassidy's real name?
A. Robert LeRoy Parker was Butch's real name.

Q. What was the Sundance Kid's real name?
A. Harry Longabaugh was the Sundance Kid's real name. (If you answered "Paul Newman" or "Robert Redford" for either of the last two questions, subtract ten points from your score.)

Q. To redeem ten points, name another famous outlaw from the Wild Bunch by alias or by actual name. Add 20 points for both.
A. Kid Curry, whose actual name was Harvey Logan, also rode with the Wild Bunch.

Q. How did Cassidy get the nickname "Butch"?
A. He worked as a butcher in Rock Springs, Wyoming for a short time in 1892. He chose the name "Cassidy" in honor of his professor in crime, Mike Cassidy.

Q. Did Butch Cassidy ever spend any time in jail?
A. Yes, he spent eighteen months in the Wyoming State Penitentiary in Laramie in 1894-95 for stealing horses.

Q. Where was Butch Cassidy born?
A. He was born in Circleville, Utah. His parents were members of the Church of Latter Day Saints, better known as Mormons.

Q. Where was the Sundance Kid born?
A. He was born in Plainfield, New Jersey, but moved to Wyoming as a child.

Q. Did the Sundance Kid ever spend any time in jail?
A. Yes, he also spent eighteen months in the Sundance, Wyoming jail for stealing horses. This is where he received his nickname.

Q. Most people have seen or at least heard of the movie, *Butch Cassidy and the Sundance Kid*, starring Paul Newman and Robert Redford. What other outlaw from the Wild Bunch had a movie made about his life?

A. Harry Tracy was a member of the Wild Bunch and a movie was made about his life.

Q. What actor played the starring role in the movie *Harry Tracy?*
A. Bruce Dern played the part.

Q. What famous songwriter/musician played a bit part as sheriff in the movie "Harry Tracy?"
A. Gordon Lightfoot played the part of a sheriff in the movie.

Q. Who was Butch and Sundance's real life female companion?
A. Etta Place was her name.

Q. In what movie did Tom Berenger and William Katt star, in 1979?
A. *Butch and Sundance: The Early Years* starred Berenger as Butch and Katt as Sundance.

Q. Is the Hole in the Wall outlaw hideout open to the public?
A. Because it is on Bureau of Land Management land, visitors may visit the Hole in the Wall Outlaw Canyon, but they must pass through private ranch property upon a designated road. Visitors will need a four-wheel-drive vehicle and must be able to hike a difficult trail.

Q. What famous Wyoming stock detective was hanged in Cheyenne on November 20, 1903 for killing a fourteen-year-old son of a sheepherder?
A. Tom Horn was hanged for this murder.

Q. What trademark sign was found at the murder scene of the sheepherder's son, Willie Nickells, that directed suspicion toward Tom Horn?
A. Two pebbles had been placed beneath the head of the murdered boy. This was known to be a Tom Horn trademark.

Q. What reason would Tom Horn have had for killing the boy?
A. Tom Horn had been hired by the cattle barons of Cheyenne to intimidate rustlers, homesteaders, and sheepherders away from occupying the open cattle range. Horn supposedly mistook the boy for his father.

Q. What famous United States marshal tricked Tom Horn into confessing to the murder of Willie Nickells, after witnessing Horn bragging in a saloon about the people that he had killed?
A. U.S. Marshal Joe LeFors arranged the confession.

Q. Who was one of Butch Cassidy and the Sundance Kid's most feared adversaries?
A. Joe LeFors was one of their frequent pursuers.

Q. Where is Joe LeFors buried?
A. Willow Grove Cemetery in Buffalo, Wyoming is the resting place of Joe LeFors.

Q. What did Tom Horn do to occupy his time while waiting in jail for his execution?
A. He braided a rope.

Q. What happened to his braiding handiwork?
A. The rope was used to hang its creator.

Q. Tom Horn made an escape attempt before he was hanged. What caused his attempt to fail?
A. He had taken a modern automatic pistol from the guard that he had overpowered. Tom Horn was not familiar with the operation of the safety on the automatic pistol, as opposed to a more familiar Colt revolver, so he was unable to fire the more modern weapon.

Q. Tom Horn's execution was quite unpopular, enough so that violence from his supporters was feared. What formidable weapon was perched on the courthouse roof to insure that the hanging would take place?
A. A Gatling gun was stationed there to keep the crowd under control.

Q. What new device was put into use at Tom Horn's hanging?
A. A water-activated trap door was used for the first time on Tom Horn's gallows. The weight of a slowly-filling water barrel tripped the trigger that held the trap door in place beneath Horn's feet.

Q. How did a hangman know the proper length of rope to use for a particular height and weight man so that the victim's neck would break instantly?
A. The hangman would most commonly consult the Army's manual on the subject. It provided a scale for men of different physiques.

Q. How long a rope was required for a six-foot-tall man of 175 pounds?
A. The rope must be 5 feet 11 inches long from the gallows beam to the prisoner's neck when he reaches the end of the drop, according to the Army manual. If the rope is too short, the man will strangle to death. If the rope is too long, the man will lose his head and the more squeamish witnesses will lose their lunch.

Q. Was Tom Horn hanged properly?
A. No, his rope was a little too short.

Q. What method of execution finally replaced the water activated gallows in Wyoming?
A. The gas chamber replaced execution by hanging in Wyoming in 1937.

Q. Was William "Buffalo Bill" Cody born on the east or the west side of the Mississippi?
A. He was born in LeClaire, Iowa on the west bank by three miles. His family soon moved to Fort Leavenworth, Kansas.

Q. What incident in his childhood caused William Cody to make his first solo trip into the western frontier?
A. At the age of twelve, William Cody stabbed a schoolmate and had to catch the next wagon train out of Fort Leavenworth until things blew over. The other boy lived and Cody was not charged.

Q. As a Pony Express Rider in Wyoming Territory in 1861, William Cody claimed he once rode from Red Buttes Station to Rocky Ridge Station and back because another rider could not ride his section after Cody's allotted section, a distance of 322 miles. How long did it take him?
A. He said he rode for 21 hours and 40 minutes. That is an average speed of 14.5 miles per hour.

Q. How many horses did he ride for the trip?
A. He rode 21 different horses—a different horse every hour.

Q. How old was Bill Cody at this time?
A. He was fourteen years old.

Q. How did Bill Cody get his job on the Pony Express?
A. He had been working as a messenger on freight wagons for the company of Russell, Majors & Waddell. Russell, Majors & Waddell created the Pony Express and Cody was Billy on the spot for the job.

Q. How many riders participated in the Pony Express?
A. About 200 hundred riders manned the Pony Express.

Q. How many horses were required to cover the route?
A. About 500 horses were required to ride the route from start to finish.

Q. How long did the fastest message take to travel the Pony Express and what was its content?
A. The news of the inauguration of Abraham Lincoln took 7 days and 17 hours to reach the end of the Pony Express.

Q. How long did the Pony Express last?
A. The Pony Express only lasted about a year and a half. The completion of the transcontinental telegraph, one year after the Pony Express began, rendered it obsolete.

Q. Did Russell, Majors & Waddell make any profits on the Pony Express?
A. No, the venture went bankrupt.

Q. Was William Cody ever an officer in the Army?
A. No, but he was a private in the Seventh Kansas Cavalry in 1864 and 1865.

Q. What other nicknames were the Seventh Kansas Cavalry known by?
A. They were known as "Jennison's Jayhawkers" or "Redlegs" by their Confederate adversaries. The Redlegs, so called because of the red leggings they wore as a mark of their unit, were noted for their heinous acts of arson, looting, and murder against civilians.

Q. Who were the antagonists in the movie *The Outlaw Josie Wales?*
A. Kansas Redlegs.

Q. How did William Cody's father die?
A. He died in 1857 from complications from being stabbed when he had spoken out in public against slavery. The family lived in Kansas at the time.

Q. What did Cody do after the Civil War?
A. He was a stagecoach driver between Fort Kearny, Nebraska and Plum Creek, Nebraska.

Q. William Cody was a married man and the father of four children. When did he get hitched?
A. He was twenty years old in 1866 when he married Louisa Frederici in St. Louis, Missouri. Although they were estranged upon his death, William Cody and Louisa remained married throughout his life.

Q. How did he support his new bride? (A clue is in a landmark in Cody, Wyoming that is named after one of his daughters.)
A. William went into the hotel business in Salt Creek Valley, Kansas. He later named his famous Irma Hotel in Cody after his daughter.

Q. How long did this business venture last?
A. He was a hotel owner for six months only at that time in his life. Then he became a scout for the Army.

Q. How did William Cody get his nickname of "Buffalo Bill"?
A. Cody hired on to the Kansas Pacific Railroad to provide buffalo meat for the construction crews.

Q. What were the wages for a railroad buffalo hunter?
A. The wages were $500 a month to bring in the hind quarters and hump of at least twelve bison a day.

Q. How many bison did Cody shoot for the railroad?
A. He shot 4,280 bison in a year and a half. This averages out to only about seven a day—maybe he took holidays and weekends off.

Q. Buffalo Bill Cody is remembered as a great scout for the Army and the producer of his famous Wild West show, but what did he spend many a winter month doing before he created the Wild West show?
A. William Cody was a well known actor in the theatres of the cities of the East Coast during the winter months.

Q. William Cody spent much of his life within the boundaries of Wyoming Territory and considered the state his home, yet he died in Denver, Colorado in 1917. Where is he buried?
A. Cody is buried on Lookout Mountain near Golden, Colorado.

Q. Why is he buried there?
A. His wife Louisa chose the plot—although most of his close associates recounted that he had wished to be buried upon Cedar Mountain, overlooking Cody, Wyoming. Buffalo Bill and Louisa were not on good terms at the end of his life.

Q. Why did the Wyoming Wool Growers' Association honor James Candlish of Rawlins, Wyoming in 1909?
A. James Candlish invented the sheepherder's wagon in 1884.

Q. What killed the Wyoming pioneer Harvey Morgan?
A. An Indian tomahawk killed Harvey Morgan.

Q. What proof is there of this cause of death?
A. His skull with the tomahawk still embedded in it is on display at the Pioneer Museum in Lander, Wyoming.

Q. How much shorter was the Bozeman Trail Cutoff than the standard Oregon Trail route through South Pass, Wyoming?
A. It was as much as 300 miles shorter, depending on the actual routes taken and the final destinations. This could save an entire month's travel which, in an area of questionable weather, could be vitally important.

Q. Where was the Bozeman Trail located?
A. The Bozeman trail began in Glenrock, Wyoming, known then as Deer Creek, and traveled northward along the eastern foothills of the Bighorn Mountains into Montana, eventually ending at Virginia City, Montana and the gold fields.

Q. Who was the Bozeman Trail named after?
A. The trail was named after a 26-year-old adventurer from Georgia, John M. Bozeman, who traveled the trail in reverse and promoted it as a better, quicker route to the Montana gold fields.

Q. Did he discover the trail?
A. No, Jim Bridger had measured the trail previously, but decided to promote a route of his own on the western side of the Bighorn Mountains instead, as a safer trail for wagon trains.

Q. What was the main drawback to using the Bozeman Trail?
A. The multiple bowstrings of the Sioux and Cheyenne Indians were drawn back to defend their chosen hunting grounds from intrusion by white settlers. The Bozeman Trail crossed land that had been set aside for the Sioux and Cheyenne by the Fort Laramie Treaty of September 17, 1851.

Q. What was the problem with Jim Bridger's trail?
A. Bridger's trail passed through a much drier landscape where water and grazing for livestock could become very scarce.

Q. How long was the Bozeman Trail used?
A. It was only used for six years. The U.S. Army abandoned the forts defending the trail in 1868.

Q. Fort Phil Kearny, the main defensive fort on the Bozeman Trail, was located near modern-day Story, Wyoming. What happened there four days before Christmas in 1866 that foreshad-

owed events that would occur ten years later in nearby Montana?
A. Captain William Fetterman and a force of eighty men were totally annihilated by Sioux and Cheyenne warriors, while trying to rescue a wood-cutting party near the fort.

Q. What had Captain Fetterman claimed that he was capable of before he was given the command to rescue the wood-cutters?
A. He had boasted that he could defeat the entire Sioux nation if he was given eighty soldiers.

Q. Was the wood-cutting party rescued?
A. Yes, the Indians ceased their attack on the wood-cutters and lured the Fetterman forces away from the fort and down over a ridge of hills where a much larger force of Indians waited in ambush. The wood-cutters returned to the fort safely.

Q. Fort Phil Kearny's commander, Colonel Henry Carrington, gave the same specific orders to Fetterman at least three times before his rescue force was allowed to leave the fort. What were those orders?
A. Carrington said, "Support the wood train, relieve it, and report to me. Do not engage or pursue the Indians at any expense. Under no circumstances pursue them over the ridge."

Q. John "Portugee" Phillips rode 235 miles to Fort Laramie to ask for immediate reinforcements after the Fetterman Massacre. How long did the ride take him?
A. He rode four days in blizzard conditions. He stopped at the telegraph office at Horseshoe Station, Wyoming to wire ahead about the disaster.

Q. What happened to the telegraph office after he left to continue on to Fort Laramie?
A. The Indians burned it down.

Q. To what secondary purpose did Phillips put the one hundred rounds of ammunition he carried on his rescue mission?
A. He strapped the ammunition to his ankles so that its weight would keep his feet in the stirrups if he dozed off while he rode.

Q. What happened to Portugee Phillips when he arrived in Fort Laramie?
A. Phillips delivered his message and fainted from exhaustion, then spent two weeks in the hospital.

Q. Was Fetterman the original officer chosen to lead the rescue party?
A. No, a veteran officer, Captain James Powell was Carrington's first choice, but Fetterman demanded to be given a chance to prove himself against the Indians.

Q. How did Captain Powell fare against a similarly large force of Indians one year later in another ambush known as the Wagon Box Fight?
A. Captain Powell had defended a makeshift corral made up of fourteen wagon boxes with fifty-three men for over four hours against some fifteen hundred Indians. When his force had been rescued by a larger group of soldiers from Fort Phil Kearny armed with a small cannon, he had lost only six men.

Q. What other factor made a significant difference in the outcome of the Wagon Box Fight, other than Powell's capable command?
A. The soldiers had been recently armed with .50 caliber repeating Springfield rifles.

Q. How many whites were killed by Indians in the vicinity of Fort Phil Kearny in the first six months of its existence?
A. One hundred and fifty-four white people were killed in that time period.

Q. What Sioux leader held military command of the Indian forces on the Bozeman Trail?
A. Red Cloud held command.

Q. What famous Sioux warrior is believed to have participated in the Fetterman Massacre?
A. Crazy Horse, a leader at the Little Bighorn Battle, is reported to have been involved in the massacre.

Q. What happened to Fort Phil Kearny, the main defensive fort on the Bozeman Trail, when the soldiers left it in 1868?

A. Red Cloud's Sioux and Cheyenne warriors immediately burned it to the ground.

Q. What did Nelson Story take up the Bozeman Trail in October of 1866?
A. Nelson Story and his cowboys drove a herd of Longhorn cattle north from Texas into Montana to start the first cattle ranching operation in the Yellowstone River area.

Q. Did Nelson Story experience trouble with the Indians?
A. The herd of 600 Texas Longhorns was detained at Fort Phil Kearny for three days because of Indian problems farther up the trail. Story's ex-Civil-War-soldier cowboys experienced little open combat with the Indians, but they did ultimately lose about half of the herd to raids.

Q. What famous television miniseries was a story about the first cattle drive from Texas to Montana?
A. *Lonesome Dove* was the television miniseries.

Q. Who won the Dull Knife Battle—U.S. cavalry or Indians?
A. The U.S. cavalry, under Col. Ranald Mackenzie, destroyed a major winter encampment of the Cheyenne Indians in a secluded valley near Kaycee, Wyoming on November 25, 1876, just a few months after the Battle of the Little Bighorn, or "Custer's Last Stand." The battle was named after Chief Dull Knife who led the Cheyenne, along with another chief, Little Wolf. This military action was part of the ongoing campaign to rid the Powder River Basin and the Black Hills of Sioux and Cheyenne occupation.

Q. "Dull Knife" was a Sioux name given to the Cheyenne chief. What was his given Cheyenne name?
A. Morning Star.

Q. Why was Mackenzie known as "Bad Hand" Mackenzie?
A. He was missing two fingers on one hand from a wound that he received during the Civil War. It was one of six wounds that he received in that war.

Q. How many Cheyenne were killed in the Dull Knife Battle?

A. The Cheyenne survivors admitted to 40 warriors killed at the initial battle. Eleven babies froze to death during the retreat over the mountains in 30-degree-below-zero weather during the following night. More Indians, men, women, and children, lost their lives on the escape route they took from the battleground up over the spine of the Bighorn Mountains in the dead of winter.

Q. Chief Little Wolf survived in spite of being shot how many times?
A. He was shot seven times.

Q. How old was he thought to have been at this time?
A. Little Wolf is believed to have been in his fifties, yet he could still outfight most of the younger braves.

Q. What did the Cheyenne survivors do to prevent some old men and women from freezing to death on the night retreat?
A. They killed some of their few remaining horses and cut the carcasses open so that the weaker refugees could put their freezing limbs inside of the hot body cavities.

Q. How many soldiers were killed?
A. One officer, Lt. John McKinney, and seven enlisted men were killed and 26 others were wounded, out of 1,200 cavalry troops.

Q. Were the government forces all white soldiers?
A. No, one third of the force consisted of Indian scouts, including two sons of the great Shoshone leader Chief Washakie. Most ironic of all, some of these Indian scouts were Sioux and Cheyenne.

Q. What was the greatest tragedy of the Dull Knife Battle?
A. Most of the remaining physical culture and art of the Northern Cheyenne people was utterly destroyed by Mackenzie and his men when they burned the nearly 200 lodges and winter stores of Dull Knife's encampment. The soldiers wished to make certain that the Cheyenne would not be able to return and resupply after the battle. Absolutely everything that was not carried away by the soldiers was destroyed.

Q. What curious items were found in the Cheyenne encampment not congruent with native culture?
A. Many items of everyday use in American culture
had been saved and used by the Cheyenne, including
china cups and plates, silverware, scissors, cooking
pots, and even pillows and mattresses.

Q. What gruesome items were found in the Cheyenne
camp that the Shoshone tribesmen felt justified their
helping the army?
A. A buckskin bag containing the right hands of twelve Shoshone
babies and the hand and arm of a Shoshone woman was found.
The Cheyenne had just returned from an attack on a Shoshone
encampment. A necklace of human fingers was also discovered,
as well as many human scalps, both Indian and white in origin.

Q. Had any of Dull Knife's warriors been involved in the Custer
or Rosebud battles earlier that year?
A. Yes, large amounts of U.S. Army supplies from Custer's 7th
Cavalry and identifiable personal effects from U. S. soldiers
were found in the village.

Q. What strange thing did some of the Cheyenne warriors do
after they finally surrendered to the U.S. Army at Red Cloud and
Spotted Tail Indian reservations much later?
A. They joined the U.S. Army as scouts to help defeat their old
allies, the Sioux.

Q. What happened to Dull Knife and Little Wolf after they eventually surrendered?
A. Dull Knife and Little Wolf, along with the remainder of their
bands, were sent to an Indian reservation in Oklahoma. The
Cheyenne did very poorly there, suffering from much sickness
and starvation. Nearly half of them died. Dull Knife and Little
Wolf led an escape over 400 miles back to Wyoming in 1878.
The two chiefs split up their band to travel faster, but both
were eventually caught. Little Wolf's group was allowed to remain in Montana. Dull Knife and his group were imprisoned, but
they escaped. Many were killed in the escape. They reached
refuge at the Pine Ridge Reservation in South Dakota and eventually joined Little Wolf in Montana.

Q. Did Col. Mackenzie participate in any other campaigns against any other Indian Tribes?
A. Most certainly yes! Col. Mackenzie had defeated Comanche Indian resistance in Texas by a similar battle in Palo Duro Canyon, Texas before he was assigned to track the Cheyenne. He had also destroyed the Comanches' essential horse herd, eliminating their ability to make war. He forced Red Cloud and his Sioux followers to settle on a reservation before the Dull Knife Battle. Later, he had much to do with the defeat and control of the Apache in New Mexico.

Q. How did Col. Ranald Mackenzie die?
A. He died thirteen years later in a mental institution, at the age of 49. He had fallen from a wagon and sustained a head injury.

Q. To what use were rifle barrels that were found on the old Dull Knife Battlefield put by the ranching family that owns the land?
A. Several were welded into a harrow to use to condition or plow the soil for planting. Others were used as gate latches.

Q. What did seven Swedes find in the southern end of the Bighorn Mountains near Kaycee, Wyoming?
A. The seven Swedes were miners from the Black Hills area. They found gold worth $7,000. Five of the seven were killed by Indians. The two escaping survivors could never find the mine again. It is known as the Lost Cabin Mine.

Q. What races of humankind were involved in the Rock Springs Massacre of September 2, 1885?
A. White coal miners attacked a neighborhood of Chinese coal miners who had been brought in by the railroad as strike breakers in Rock Springs, Wyoming.

Q. How many Chinese were injured or killed in the raid on Rock Springs' Chinatown?
A. 28 Chinese were killed and 15 wounded.

Q. Was anyone ever brought to justice for the crimes committed in the massacre?
A. No, sixteen men were arrested and imprisoned in a Green

River jail, but none was brought to trial and no punishment or sentences were ever issued.

Q. How many people were killed in Wyoming's largest coal mine disaster at Hana, Wyoming in 1903?

A. The mine explosion killed 171 people.

Q. How many people died in the second-largest coal mining disaster on August 14, 1923 at Kemmerer, Wyoming?
A. One hundred people died in the mine explosion.

Q. How did the Flaming Gorge, a spectacular canyon area that lies south of Rock Springs, Wyoming, receive its name?
A. John Wesley Powell, the first explorer of the Grand Canyon, named the canyon for its brilliantly colored sunlit walls. He began his exploration of the Colorado River system on the Green River in Wyoming. A granite marker stands in the town of Green River's Expedition Island Park to mark the spot of his departure.

Q. What disability did John Wesley Powell have?
A. He was missing an arm. He lost it at the Battle of Shiloh in the Civil War.

Q. The Indians called the Green River Seeds-ke-dee. What did this mean?
A. It meant "prairie hen" in the Crow language.

Q. What sparked the Mormon War of 1857?
A. President James Buchanan appointed Alfred Cumming to replace the Mormon leader, Brigham Young, as the Utah territorial governor. This caused a great discord among the largely Mormon inhabitants of Utah Territory. Buchanan sent two-thirds of the United States Army to Utah to enforce the change and Cumming's authority.

Q. Did the Mormons have an army of their own?
A. Yes, they raised a militia called the Nauvoo Legion.

Q. What did "Nauvoo" signify?
A. Nauvoo, Illinois was the original settlement for the Mormons when they left New York State. "Nauvoo" is a Hebrew word meaning "beautiful plantation."

Q. Who won the battle?
A. No battle ever occurred. The two armies never met. The Nauvoo Legion did manage to burn down two U.S. forts, Fort Bridger and Fort Supply. Tensions eventually eased without further conflict.

Q. What took the place of the huge herds of bison in Wyoming, after their destruction?
A. Large herds of Texas Longhorn cattle were brought into the empty grasslands by wealthy cattle barons.

Q. Of what nationality were most of the cattle barons of Wyoming?
A. Over half of the cattle barons were from England or Scotland.

Q. Were these wealthy foreigners cowboys?
A. No, most of the cattle barons only provided the money and business know-how. They hired local cowboys to run their ranches.

Q. Did the barons own the land?
A. While the barons did own large parcels of land around their ranches, most of the land utilized for grazing was public land or open range.

Q. Did the cattle barons spend most of their time at the ranches overseeing operations?
A. No, the hired foremen usually oversaw running the ranches. The cattle barons lived at their mansions in Cheyenne and visited their ranches as exotic wilderness retreats. Wealthy guests were often brought to the ranches for extended parties and holidays.

Q. How did the guests travel to the ranches from the eastern United States?
A. They rode the new railroads to Denver and then took elaborate stagecoach journeys of over two hundred miles to reach the ranches.

Q. What famous landmark in Cheyenne did the cattle baron families use as their unofficial country club?
A. The Cheyenne Club was the center of the cattle baron society.

Q. When was the Cheyenne Club built?
A. The Cheyenne Club was constructed in 1881.

Q. How much did the Cheyenne Club cost to build?
A. The Cheyenne Club cost $25,000 to construct, or about $30 million in today's value.

Q. What was the total number of members allowed to be long to the Cheyenne Club?
A. Two hundred members was the limit of the Cheyenne Club roster.

Q. How many cattle were shipped per day in the autumn of 1883 on the Union Pacific Railroad from Wyoming?
A. One hundred railroad carloads of cattle per day left Wyoming in 1883. At perhaps 25 cattle per car, that is 2,500 head per day.

Q. The Swan Land and Cattle Company, located near Chugwater, Wyoming, was one of the largest cattle ranching businesses in Wyoming during the 1880s. How many cattle did it have on its records in 1885?
A. Over 100,000 cattle were supposedly owned by the Swan Land and Cattle Company.

Q. How much land did this cattle company control?
A. It controlled an area the size of Connecticut.

Q. How many cattle did the Swan Land and Cattle Company own after the severe winter of 1886-1887?
A. The company owned about 57,000 living cattle.

Q. Did all of these cattle die in the winter cold?
A. No. Although many of the cattle starved or froze to death in the bitter winter, it was discovered that someone had "cooked the books" so that the company had appeared to have many more assets than were actually on the hoof.

Q. How were these records altered?
A. When the cattle were driven through a corral to be counted, they were simply circled around a hill and driven before the naive cattle counter a second and third time.

Q. Where were the owners of the Swan Land and Cattle Company from?
A. The owners were from Scotland.

Q. Can a person visit the Swan Land and Cattle Company ranch today?
A. Yes, it is a National Historical Landmark near Chugwater, Wyoming.

Q. What famous cattle detective turned assassin, and the subject of at least two movies (one starring Steve McQueen) worked for the Swan Land and Cattle Company at one time?
A. Tom Horn worked as a cattle detective for the Swan Land and Cattle Company in 1893.

Q. Who made up the two sides of the conflict in the Johnson County War of Wyoming in 1891?
A. The Wyoming Stock Growers Association, composed of wealthy large-ranch owners made up one side; the Northern Wyoming Farmers and Stock Growers Association, made up of smaller ranchers from the area around Buffalo, Wyoming, formed the other side.

Q. What were these two groups fighting over?
A. The official reason was that the large ranch owners based in the southern part of Wyoming felt that the smaller ranchers were rustling their new, unbranded calves to supplement the small ranchers' own herds. Actually, the members of the Wyoming Stock Growers Association wished to gain exclusive control of the rich grazing lands along the east face of the Bighorn Mountains.

Q. What natural occurrence also contributed to the causes of the Johnson County War?
A. Severe blizzards in the winter of 1886-1887 greatly decreased the cattle herds of Wyoming.

Many large cattle barons went out of business, while smaller cattle ranchers who lived off the land had better chances of survival. The surviving cattle barons could ill afford to have the small ranchers restock their herds by branding new "maverick" calves that may have belonged to the cattle barons' herds.

Q. If this conflict was known as a war, who were the soldiers?
A. The Wyoming Stock Growers hired 21 gunfighters from Texas and seven local stock detectives to accompany 21 of the Association's members on an invasion of the Johnson County area. Eventually, the Northern Wyoming Farmers and Stock Growers Association were represented by Buffalo's sheriff, Red Angus, and two hundred volunteers.

Q. What Indian trick did the invaders use to keep the Johnson County ranchers from knowing about their impending attack?
A. The invaders cut the telegraph wires into the area.

Q. How many battles took place in the Johnson County War?
A. Two battles occurred. One conflict took place at the KC Ranch, located in Kaycee, Wyoming about forty miles south of Buffalo. The other battle took place at the TA Ranch near Buffalo.

Q. Which side won the battle at KC?
A. The invading force from southern Wyoming, composed of over fifty men, surrounded two prominent rustlers from Johnson County in a ranch building at the KC Ranch and killed them. One man, Nick Ray was shot almost immediately. The other man held off his attackers for nine hours until they burned him out and shot him.

Q. What was the name of this tragic champion of Johnson County?
A. Nate Champion was his name.

Q. What did the victors leave with Nate Champion's body?
A. They pinned a note to his corpse saying "Cattle thieves, Beware."

Q. Nate Champion kept a journal of the day's events as he held the regulators at bay at the TA Ranch. What was the last entry in the diary?

A. He wrote, "It is not night yet. The house is all fired. Good-bye boys, if I never see you again."

Q. Which side won the battle at TA?
A. The battle was a stand-off between the forces from the south, which were holed up in the TA ranch buildings and the 200-man army from Buffalo, led by Red Angus. The ensuing battle lasted three days until the U.S. Cavalry arrived from Fort McKinney in Buffalo to stop the conflict after the telegraph wires had been repaired.

Q. What ingenious device did Red Angus intend to use against the defenders at the TA Ranch?
A. The Johnson County forces had constructed a moving defense wall by affixing two layers of eight-inch-thick logs between two wagons. The whole assembly was to be pushed forward, close enough to throw dynamite into the ranch compound.

Q. Where did the dynamite come from?
A. The Johnson County forces had captured the southern invaders' supply wagons, which contained the dynamite.

Q. What did the cavalry do?
A. They placed forty-nine of the southern regulators under arrest and eventually took them south to Fort Russell in Cheyenne. Most were held there for nearly three years, but were later released without charges when Johnson County could no longer afford to pay room and board for so many prisoners. Nevertheless, the power of the wealthy southern ranchers had been broken in Johnson County. (Rumor has it that Red Angus had a successful career in the fledgling World Wrestling Association. Poor Nate Champion did not survive for such an illustrious career.)

Q. What is the name of a popular breed of cattle that is now raised in many parts of Wyoming?
A. By coincidence only, Red Angus is a breed commonly raised in Wyoming.

Q. Does the Wyoming Stock Growers Association still exist?
A. Yes, it is alive and thriving, but the Northern Wyoming Farmers and Stock Growers Association is gone.

Q. What governor and United States senator from Wyoming began his rise to wealth and influence from a life as a young Texas cowboy?
A. Senator John Kendrick left Texas in 1879 to help drive cattle to the prairies of Wyoming.

Q. Did the fierce winter of 1886-1887 ruin John Kendrick's cattle operation?
A. No, in fact, the winter weakened the large cattle operations enough to allow Kendrick, a small but savvy cattle rancher, to buy his way into and ultimately purchase the much larger Converse Cattle Company.

Q. Did John Kendrick gain his wealth in the cattle business alone?
A. No, he moved the Converse Cattle Company to northern Wyoming with its operations center in Sheridan. He became an entrepreneur involved in several of the businesses of Sheridan, but ranching remained his first love.

Q. What is the name of his home in Sheridan?
A. His grand mansion rises from the top of a high bluff in the center of Sheridan. He named it "Trail End." Now a State Historic Site, it can be toured by the public.

Q. How many terms did John Kendrick serve as governor?
A. He only served two years of a four-year term. He was elected to the United States Senate before completing his governorship.

Q. What is unique about his election in Wyoming history?
A. Kendrick was the first popularly elected senator. Before this time, senators had been elected by the members of state senates.

Q. How many terms did he serve as a U.S. senator?
A. He served three terms as a senator.

Q. Was he defeated for a fourth term?
A. No, he chose not to seek reelection. John Kendrick died in 1933, before his third term was quite complete.

Q. Who was the only person to hold the office of Governor of Wyoming for three terms?
A. Governor Ed Herschler was elected to the office for three terms. He served from 1975 to 1987.

Q. What was Governor Herschler's political party?
A. He was a Democrat.

Q. What is the predominant political party in Wyoming?
A. Wyoming is a largely Republican state.

Q. Has European royalty ever visited Wyoming?
A. Yes, Queen Elizabeth II of England visited Sheridan, Wyoming in 1964, where she actually shopped for herself for the first time in her privileged and protected life.

Q. When did the first airplane arrive in Wyoming?
A. The first airplane arrived in Gillette, Wyoming in 1911.

Q. Did it land safely?
A. The plane did not land at all. It was shipped to Gillette in a box car. George Thompson flew his plane safely away from Gillette.

Q. What famous aviator landed a plane in Gillette in 1916?
A. Charles Lindbergh landed a plane in Gillette in 1916.

Q. What famous aviator had plans to build a cabin on a mining claim near Meeteetse, Wyoming?
A. Amelia Earhart had visited the area and wished to live there.

Q. What prevented her from finishing her cabin?
A. She was lost over the Pacific Ocean on her attempt to complete a flight around the world.

Q. What is the Tie Hack Memorial near Dubois, Wyoming honoring?
A. The Tie Hack Memorial honors the hard work of the lumbermen who hacked railroad ties from the Wyoming wilderness for the building of the railroads. This was a big local industry in the late 1800s and early 1900s.

Q. Of what nationalities were most of the tie hacks?
A. Most tie hacks were from the Scandinavian countries of Norway, Sweden, and Finland.

Q. How many railroad ties were harvested in a good year at the turn of the 20th Century?
A. The tie hackers could ship over 400,000 railroad ties in a good year.

Q. How many ties were required to set one mile off track?
A. 2,500 ties were required for one mile of track.

Q. How many ties could a good tie hack hack in a day if a tie hack could hack ties?
A. A good tie hack could hack over 300 in a day in 1930, when more power tools were available.

Q. How much was he paid per tie?
A. Three cents a tie.

Q. Were the ties all used in Wyoming?
A. No, most went to the midwestern states where suitable trees were seldom available.

Q. A water-filled wooden flume extended down the Tongue River Canyon from high in the Bighorn Mountains a distance of ten miles to the town of Ranchester. How long did it take a log to cover this distance in the flume?
A. Nine minutes—logs reached speeds well over sixty miles per hour.

ARTS AND LITERATURE

Q. What famous "splatter painting" artist of the middle 20th Century was born in Cody, Wyoming?
A. Jackson Pollock was born in Cody, but he and his family moved from there when he was only an infant.

Q. What famous realistic painter of the Old West lives in Wapiti, Wyoming?
A. James Bama.

Q. What art works did James Bama first become known for?
A. He illustrated mid-20th-Century editions of action novels such as *Doc Savage* and *Tarzan*.

Q. What well-known illustrator of paperback books also lived in Cody, Wyoming?
A. Nick Eggenhofer lived and practiced in Cody. He was known as the "King of the Pulps" for his prolific illustrations of paperback books.

Q. Where was Nick Eggenhofer born?
A. He was born in Germany in 1897. He died in Cody in 1985.

Q. What Cody, Wyoming-based artist had his beginnings in the Chicago mafia empire of Al Capone?
A. World-renowned artist Harry Jackson was born into the Shapiro family in Chicago, an integral part of Al Capone's crime empire.

Q. Did Harry Jackson benefit from his relationship to Capone's mafia?
A. Not at all, in fact Mr. Jackson fled Chicago at the age of fourteen to Wyoming. He has used his mother's maiden name ever since.

Q. Did Harry Jackson become a practicing artist right away in Wyoming?
A. No, he worked as a cowboy, a big-game guide, and in other outdoor-related occupations.

Q. How did Harry Jackson really get his start in the art world?
A. Jackson joined the Marines and fought in the front lines in the Pacific Theater. One of his official positions was that of a sketch artist for his battalion. After being wounded several times, he was stationed stateside and appointed the official Marine Corps artist.

Q. In what medium does Harry Jackson work?
A. Mr. Jackson is most noted for his realistic bronzes of western subject matter. He has worked in many styles and media, most notably abstract expressionism.

Q. What is unique about Harry Jackson's bronze sculptures?
A. Harry Jackson paints them in vivid color, much as the ancient Greeks painted their marbles.

Q. What famous cowboy actor has been the close friend and subject matter of Harry Jackson's work?
A. The figure of John Wayne astride a stallion was created for the Great Western Financial Corporation of Beverly Hills, California.

Q. How tall is the sculpture of John Wayne?
A. The sculpture stands 21 feet high in front of the corporate offices.

Q. What connection does Harry Jackson have to modern avionics?
A. One of Harry Jackson's six ex-wives is the daughter of Bill Lear, the inventor of the Lear jet.

Q. Did Harry Jackson ever meet Jackson Pollock?
A. Yes, they were close friends.

Q. What Shell, Wyoming artist is known for her nearly photo-realistic paintings of horses and ranch people?
A. Ann Hanson.

Q. What Wyoming artist's watercolor paintings have been described as "tropical western wildlife"?
A. The wildlife paintings of Sarah Rogers depict Wyoming wildlife in vibrant colors, instead of the usual muted, natural tones.

Q. What Jackson Hole artist not only likes to paint portraits of mountains and the people who inhabit them, but also likes to climb the mountains?
A. Dave McNally.

Q. What Casper, Wyoming artist lost the use of his arms and legs in a rodeo accident and now paints using a mouthpiece to hold his brushes?
A. Barry Reed.

Q. What Riverton, Wyoming artist is known as the "Quilting Cowgirl"?
A. Marta Amundson.

Q. What is the subject matter of the imagery incorporated in Marta Amundson's quilts?
A. She portrays wildlife and nature to bring awareness about environmental issues to public view.

Q. What prestigious award did Marta Amundson win in 2001?
A. She won the American Folk Art Museum International Spirit of Design Competition.

Q. What Wyoming artist has created ornaments for a White House Christmas tree for President Clinton?
A. Laurie Thal created glass ornaments at her Wilson, Wyoming studio for a White House Christmas tree during Bill Clinton's presidency.

Q. Does Laurie Thal create only ornaments at her glass-blowing studio?

A. No, she mainly creates one-of-a-kind glass vessels. The ornaments were requested by Hillary Clinton.

Q. What other Wyoming artist often collaborates with Laurie Thal on her blown-glass vessels by sandblasting unique designs into their surfaces?
A. Lia Kass is often asked to enhance Laurie Thal's creations with her sand-blasted designs.

Q. What Wyoming saddle maker is acknowledged as one of the finest and most influential saddle crafters in the world?
A. Don King, owner of King's Saddlery, is internationally known as a creator of some of the most beautiful western saddles.

Q. What is distinctive about a Don King's saddles and other Sheridan-style saddles?
A. The saddles are embellished with extensive floral patterns carved and stamped into the leather.

Q. Where can a person view over 500 examples of the saddle making craft?
A. A visitor to Sheridan, Wyoming can view over 500 saddles at the King's Saddlery Museum, which is located behind the King's Saddlery store.

Q. What Wyoming poet worked for forty years as a reporter for the Associated Press?
A. W. Dale Nelson.

Q. What Wyoming poet has written poetry collections including *Croutons on a Cow Pie,* among other works?
A. Baxter Black.

Q. What was Baxter Black's previous profession?
A. He was a veterinarian.

Q. What Wyoming author has won the prestigious Nebula Award for science-fiction?
A. Edward Winslow Bryant, Jr.

Q. What Wyoming author, who specialized in Wyoming history, was an expert on wool and worked with the United States government and Chinese government to improve the quality of wool-growing in both countries?
A. Robert Homer Burns.

Q. What Shell, Wyoming author was greatly inspired in her career after being struck by lightning?
A. Gretel Ehrlich was on a walk with her dog when she was struck by lightning. She wrote about the experience in her book *A Match to the Heart*, which became one of her best-selling books.

Q. After being struck by lightning, Gretel Ehrlich was advised to go to a place of lower altitude than her home in Wyoming. Where did she go?
A. She went to Greenland to live with the Inuit people and research a book.

Q. Did she write about the experience?
A. Yes, she wrote a book entitled *This Cold Heaven*.

Q. Has Gretel Ehrlich written any books about Wyoming?
A. Yes, she wrote a book entitled *The Solace of Open Spaces* about living in Wyoming.

Q. Gretel Ehrlich wrote another book about a major location in Wyoming related to World War II. The book bears the name of that location. Name the book.
A. The book is entitled *Heart Mountain*.

Q. What book by Wyoming author Joe Back is known as the packer's bible by outfitters?
A. *Horses, Hitches, and Rocky Trails.*

Q. What true crime story that occurred in Casper, Wyoming is Ron Franscell's book *Fall* about?
A. *Fall* is about the murder of two teenage sisters in Casper, Wyoming in 1973.

Q. Why did Ron Franscell choose to write about this crime?
A. The sisters had been his neighbors and childhood friends in Casper.

Q. How were the girls murdered?
A. They were thrown from a high bridge after the older sister was raped. Actually, the older sister survived the murder attempt, but was so traumatized by the event that she returned to the bridge eighteen years later and jumped to her death.

Q. Were the two men ever caught and prosecuted for the crimes?
A. Yes, both were caught and sentenced to death, but the sentence was later commuted to life imprisonment. One man died in prison; the other still lives.

Q. What other books has Ron Franscell written?
A. He has written two works of fiction: *Angel Fire* and *The Deadline*.

Q. What two Wyoming authors live on bison ranch in the Owl Mountains of central Wyoming?
A. The married couple of Michael and Kathleen O'Neal Gear live and work on their Red Canyon Ranch, where they also raise bison.

Q. Michael Gear has been nominated for what two prestigious awards in his writing career?
A. He has been nominated for the Pulitzer Prize in fiction and the National Book Award in 1998 for his novel *Morning River*.

Q. How many novels has Michael Gear written?
A. He has written twelve novels.

Q. Do Michael and Kathleen Gear ever write books together?
A. Yes, they have written seventeen novels together. The works of both authors are based on archeology, history, and prehistory.

Q. What Wyoming author wrote about her childhood in a large Mormon household and her life as the wife of a Wyoming game warden?

A. Hunter Rodello wrote about Mormon life in her book *House of Many Rooms: A Family Memoir*. In *Wyoming Wife*, she wrote about life with her game warden husband, Frank Caulkins.

Q. What Jackson Hole, Wyoming author has had his books about teenagers made into movies with titles such as *Floating Away* and *Skipped Parts?*
A. Tim Sandlin wrote the books and the screenplays.

Q. What unusual odd jobs has Tim Sandlin held while he was practicing his writing career?
A. He has driven an ice cream truck, skinned elk, and buffed belt buckles.

Q. What did he use for a home during much of his early writing career?
A. Tim Sandlin resided in a tent or a tepee, pitched on public land, for many years.

Q. What Cheyenne, Wyoming author writes detective novels featuring a fictitious Wyoming game warden named Joe Pickett as the sleuth?
A. *Savage Run*, *Winter Kill*, and *Trophy Hunt* are all books by C. J. Box, which feature the main character Joe Pickett.

Q. What Wyoming outdoor activities training institute did both Sebastian Junger, the author of *The Perfect Storm*, and David Morell, the author of *First Blood (Rambo)* graduate from?
A. Both authors graduated from the National Outdoor Leadership School in Lander, Wyoming.

Q. How did the town of Parkman, Wyoming get its name?
A. Parkman is named after Francis Parkman, historian and author of *The Oregon Trail*. He visited this area of Wyoming that the Bozeman Trail cutoff from the Oregon Trail had passed through.

Q. What Glenrock, Wyoming artisan creates suits of medieval armor of museum quality?
A. Travis Blankenbaker creates suits of armor that are historically accurate and fully functional.

Q. Can an individual order a personal suit of armor created by Travis Blankenbaker?
A. Yes, for a price. Suits of armor may start at $2,500, and increase in cost as quality and options are added. Travis Blankenbaker created a pair of historically accurate Roman greaves or shin guards for a customer for $600.

Q. Does anyone use the suits of armor that Travis Blankebaker creates?
A. Yes, Travis and other members of the Casper, Wyoming chapter of the Society for Creative Anachronism wear the armor in combat competition. Travis made a highly ornamental suit of armor to wear to his own wedding. He does not wear this suit in combat.

Q. According to Travis, which type of armor protects its wearer better against the blunt wooden practice combat swords used by Society for Creative Anachronism contestants: chain mail or plate steel?
A. When struck by the rattan sword, a contestant wearing chain mail will suffer broken bones. A contestant wearing plate steel will only sustain bruises.

Q. What medieval apparel does Travis's wife Robyn create?
A. Robyn Blankenbaker creates medieval dresses.

Q. Robyn created her own medieval wedding dress. The dress was adorned with 1,000 of what object?
A. She sewed over 1,000 pearls to her dress, along with other beading and ornamentation.

Q. What would be the cost of such a dress to a potential customer?
A. At least $700.

Q. How much time was required to create the wedding dress?
A. Four months.

Q. How many layers actually compose a medieval dress?
A. Two layers actually make up a medieval lady's garment: an underdress and an overdress. Multiple layers of petticoats and pantaloons were worn beneath the dress.

Q. Medieval dresses were composed of what materials?
A. Linen was a common fabric. Silks and satins were also used on court dresses.

Q. What sinister accessory would no medieval lady be caught without?
A. Women commonly carried daggers somewhere on their person. The weapon might be worn in the belt that all ladies wore, or it might be concealed in the boot. Daggers sometimes were even concealed in the bodice if the cleavage was ample.

Q. What rhinestone-bedecked singer/composer from the 1960s and '70s spent a large part of his childhood in Cheyenne, Wyoming?
A. Neil Diamond spent some years as a child in Cheyenne because his father was stationed at Warren Air Force Base.

Q. What three-person group, based in southern Wyoming, performs orally recited poetry in three synchronized parts like a choral presentation without music?
A. Stephanie Painter, George Vlastos, and Jim Gaither make up the poetry performance group WordBand. Their performance material may be taken from well known poets, works of their own creation, or sources as eclectic as newspaper articles.

Q. What was the title of the first book published in Wyoming?
A. *Dictionary of the Sioux Language* by Charles Guerren was the first book published in Wyoming.

Q. When was it published?
A. The book was published in 1852.

Q. Where was it published?
A. The book was published at Fort Laramie.

Q. What famous western novel, which spawned several movies and a television series of the late 1960s, was set in and around the town of Medicine Bow, Wyoming in 1902, by Owen Wister?
A. *The Virginian.*

Q. Where was Owen Wister from?
A. Philadelphia, Pennsylvania.

Q. What was his educational background?
A. He held degrees from Harvard in music and law.

Q. What led to Owen Wister's interest in the western culture of Wyoming?
A. He spent much time in Wyoming due to a need for a drier climate for his health. A monument honoring Owen Wister can be viewed in Medicine Bow.

Q. What famous line does the Virginian speak when he is called a foul name by his opponent in a card game?
A. The Virginian draws his pistol and says, "When you call me that, *smile!*" Owen Wister may have actually heard Carbon County Deputy Sheriff James Davis speak this line to a fellow player in a card game.

Q. What is the Virginian's real name?
A. No one knows. It is never given in the book.

Q. Gary Cooper played the part of the Virginian in a movie version in 1929. Who was his dialogue coach?
A. Randolph Scott, future star of many movies of his own, but who had not yet begun acting, served as his dialogue coach.

Q. What famous actor who portrayed an American president in *Independence Day* also directed and portrayed the lead role in a remake of *The Virginian* for Turner Broadcasting System?
A. Bill Pullman became the most recent Virginian in a television production of *The Virginian* in 2000.

Q. What book did Wyoming author Mary O'Hara write that became a movie and a television series?
A. She wrote *My Friend Flicka*, a book about a girl and her horse.

Q. How many languages has *My Friend Flicka* been translated into?
A. It has been translated into sixty-two languages.

Q. What American landscape artist's rustic studio cabin may be toured in Dayton, Wyoming?
A. The studio cabin of Hans Kleiber may be visited in Dayton.

Q. Hans Kleiber was born in Cologne, Germany and lived to the age of 80. How many of those years did he live in Wyoming?
A. Hans Kleiber lived in Wyoming for 61 years.

Q. Where was the first county public library established in the United States?
A. The first county library was established in Cheyenne, Wyoming in 1886.

Q. What well known female author of mystery novels spent many summers at the Eaton Dude Ranch near Sheridan, Wyoming?
A. Mary Roberts Rinehart spent many summers at the Eaton Ranch. She was a prolific writer of mystery and detective novels.

Q. What famous phrase, intrinsic to murder mysteries, came from Mary Roberts Rinehart's novel, *The Door*?
A. "The butler did it," is the famous phrase from *The Door*.

Q. In the novel, *The Door*, did the butler do it?
A. Yes.

Q. Mary Roberts Rinehart wrote her mysteries in the "scientific detection" style. What popular television series, set in Las Vegas, Miami, and New York, is the direct descendant of this style? (Clue: Horatio, Gil)
A. The *CSI* television series are direct descendants of "scientific detection" novels.

Q. Who was a contemporary female murder mystery writer from England that was not as famous as Mary Roberts Rinehart during her time, but has since become a household name?
A. Agatha Christie was a contemporary of Mary Roberts Rinehart, and wrote *Murder on the Orient Express* and many other well-known crime thrillers.

Q. Where did Ernest Hemingway finish his novel *A Farewell to Arms?*
A. Ernest Hemingway finished *A Farewell to Arms* at a dude ranch named Spear-O-Wigwam located high in the Bighorn Mountains near Sheridan, Wyoming.

Q. Where did Spear-O-Wigwam get its name?
A. The dude ranch was created by Wyoming Senator Willis Spear and his family in 1920. The main guest lodge of the ranch was created from lodge pole pines to resemble a huge Indian wigwam.

Q. Does Spear-O-Wigwam still exist?
A. Yes, the dude ranch resort is still in business and flourishing. Hemingway's cabin also still exists and is available to customers.

Q. What Wyoming author was instrumental in the creation of the Wilderness Act and the establishment of the Arctic National Wildlife Refuge?
A. Margaret Murie was known as the "grandmother of the conservation movement" and was the main proponent of the Wilderness Act and the Arctic National Wildlife Refuge in Alaska. She lived in Moose, Wyoming.

Q. What honor did President Bill Clinton bestow upon Margaret Murie in 1998?
A. He awarded her the Presidential Medal of Freedom.

Q. What is the title of Margaret Murie's book about life in Moose, Wyoming?
A. *Wapiti Wilderness.*

Q. Who illustrated *Wapiti Wilderness?*
A. Her husband, Olaus Murie, illustrated the book. He was also a prime mover in the wilderness preservation movement.

Q. What late-19th-Century humorist was the first editor and manager of the *Laramie Boomerang?*
A. Edgar Wilson "Bill" Nye was the first editor of the *Boomerang.*

Q. What was the *Boomerang* named after?
A. The *Boomerang* was named after Bill Nye's mule.

Q. What was Bill Nye's original occupation?
A. He was a lawyer, but his practice was so unsuccessful that he often could not afford coal to heat his office, nor postage for his outgoing mail.

Q. Where can a person view a large collection of western art in an original, restored ranch house?
Q. A fine collection of western art, including many works by Charlie Russell and Frederic Remington, can be seen at the Bradford Brinton Memorial Museum near Big Horn, Wyoming.

Q. What was the original name of the ranch that contains the Bradford Brinton Memorial Museum?
A. The ranch was known as the Quarter Circle A Ranch.

Q. Why is the Bradford Brinton Museum located on the Quarter Circle A Ranch?
A. Bradford Brinton bought the ranch from the Moncreiffe family in 1923. He was a collector of fine western art. Upon his death, his sister, Helen, created the museum. The grounds are listed on the National Register of Historic Places and may be viewed by the public.

Q. Did Bradford Brinton start the Quarter Circle A Ranch?
A. No, a wealthy pair of Scottish brothers, William and Malcolm Moncreiffe, began the ranch as a cattle operation in the early 1890s.

Q. Did the Moncreiffes participate in the polo activities in Big Horn?
A. Most certainly yes; they held the first matches at the Quarter Circle A. The two raised some of the finest polo ponies in the world.

Q. What other types of horses for specialized use did the Moncreiffes export from the Quarter Circle A?
A. They sold horses to the British cavalry for use in the Boer War in South Africa.

Q. How many museums are actually housed in the Buffalo Bill Historical Center of Cody, Wyoming?
A. There are five international-quality museums housed in the Buffalo Bill Historical Center. They are the Buffalo Bill Museum, the Whitney Gallery of Western Art, the Plains Indian Museum, the Cody Firearms Museum, and the Draper Museum of Natural History.

Q. Name any famous western artist whose work can be found in the Whitney Gallery of Western Art.
A. Any of the big three of Frederic Remington, Charlie Russell, or George Catlin would suffice as an answer. Many other famous artists are also represented there.

Q. Can other exhibits of art be found in the BBHC other than the Whitney Gallery of Western Art?
A. Yes. Actually, one museum seems to flow into the next. The Buffalo Bill Museum is filled with posters from the wild west show, portraits, and related art works. It is impossible to separate art from the artifacts of the daily lives of the Native Americans in the Plains Indian Museum. The manufacturing of firearms, especially in its earlier history, is an art form in itself. The Draper Museum is also full of sculptures and landscapes.

Q. Who is represented by the large bronze statue located to the right and rear of the BBHC?
A. Buffalo Bill himself, of course. The statue is known as the Buffalo Bill Monument.

Q. What is the name of his mount? (hint: A bear also once bore this name.)
A. The horse was named Smokey.

Q. Who created this sculpture?
A. Gertrude Vanderbilt Whitney created the Buffalo Bill Monument.

Q. Was Mrs. Whitney a starving artist?
A. No, she was part of wealthy American society both through bloodline and marriage. She was born into the famously wealthy Vanderbilt family and married Harry Payne Whitney, whose family owned Standard Oil Company, among other things.

Q. What unique insight into artist's lives can be found within the Whitney Gallery of Western Art?
A. Three reconstructed artists' studios, those of Frederic Remington, W. H. D. Koerner, and Joseph Henry Sharp, can be viewed within the gallery.

Q. What artist created a large mural upon the ceiling of the Mormon Chapel in Cody, Wyoming?
A. Edward T. Grigware created the mural in 1951.

Q. Was this Mr. Grigware's first trip to Cody?
A. No, Grigware had relocated to Cody several years before as part of an effort to found an artists' colony near the Buffalo Bill Historical Center.

Q. Can this mural be viewed by the general public?
A. Yes.

Q. Is there anywhere else in Cody that Mr. Grigware's art can be viewed?
A. Yes, a painting of his hangs in the Bottoms Up Lounge of the Holiday Inn.

Q. Where else in the world are Mr. Grigware's works located?
A. His works can be viewed in the Mormon Temple of Los Angeles, California, and in Hawaii at the Brigham Young University.

Q. Was Mr. Grigware a member of the Church of Latter Day Saints?
A. No, he was Catholic.

Q. What subject matter did Edward Grigware paint other than western scenes?
A. During World War II he served as a recruiting artist for the Navy. He painted many scenes of naval operations in the Aleutian Islands in Alaska.

Q. What other artist accompanied Edward Grigware from Chicago to Cody to form an artists' colony?
A. A photographer named Stanley Kershaw also moved from Chicago to Cody, Wyoming.

Q. A large sculpture of an Indian's head stands in front of the Washakie County Courthouse in Worland, Wyoming. Is this the only one of its kind in the world?
A. No, the sculpture, entitled "Trail of Whispering Giants" is one of sixty-seven currently located throughout the United States and Canada.

Q. Who created the sculptures?
A. Artist Peter Wolf Toth created the sculpture in Worland, as well as all of the others. He gave it to the State of Wyoming to honor the Native American residents.

Q. Is Peter Wolf Toth from Wyoming?
A. No, he was born in Hungary and now resides in Orlando, Florida.

Q. What is the sculpture made of?
A. The sculpture is carved from a Douglas fir that was over 260 years old. The tree came from the small town of Hyattville, Wyoming, located a few miles north of Worland.

Q. What number in the series of sixty-seven is the Worland sculpture?
A. It is Number 39.

Q. What early photographer helped inspire the approval of Yellowstone as the first national park?
A. The photographs of William Henry Jackson, taken in the future Yellowstone Park in 1871 helped inspire the creation of the world's first national park in Yellowstone.

Q. In 1871, the process of developing photographs from glass plates was very time consuming. What natural wonder helped William H. Jackson speed up the developing process in Yellowstone Park?
A. He utilized 160-degree water from the hot springs to double the speed of the reaction time of his developing chemicals.

Q. What incident caused the loss of a month's photographic efforts for Jackson?

A. A mule carrying the glass plates stumbled and rolled, breaking up the glass plates.

Q. What artist's photographs of elk in Jackson Hole, Wyoming at the turn of the 20th Century helped bring the drastic decline of the country's elk population to the public's attention?
A. The photographs by Stephen Leek gained national attention and helped bring about measures to create refuges for elk and to control elk hunting so that their numbers could increase to healthy populations.

Q. What in particular were elk killed for, much as buffalo were killed for their hides?
A. Elk were killed in large numbers for their ivory teeth, to be used in jewelry.

Q. What were the hunters called who killed elk for their teeth?
A. The hunters were known as "tuskers."

Q. What other point of interest pertaining to Native American Art can be found in Hyattville?
A. The Medicine Lodge Archaeological Site near Hyattville features a stunning cliff face covered with petroglyphs and pictographs, which can be viewed by the public at nearly arm's length.

Q. What is a petroglyph?
A. A petroglyph is a design carved into the rock, much as a relief sculpture is done.

Q. What is a pictograph?
A. A pictograph is a design painted or stained onto the rock wall.

Q. How long have people inhabited the Medicine Lodge area?
A. Archeologists have uncovered evidence that humans occupied the site for over ten thousand years.

Q. Where did the paint come from that was first used to cover the Brooklyn Bridge in New York City?
A. A pigment known as Rawlins Red came from a paint mine near Rawlins, Wyoming. A boxcar load was required to cover the bridge.

Q. What is the Neltje Blanchan Memorial Award given for?
A. This $1,000 award is presented annually by the Wyoming Arts Council to an outstanding new author. The author must be a Wyoming resident, have published no more than one book, and not have received the award in the previous four years. The work submitted must be inspired by nature in some way. This award is funded by Neltje Blanchan's granddaughter, also named Neltje.

Q. What is the Frank Nelson Doubleday Award given for?
A. This award is also a $1,000 award given by the Wyoming Arts Council with the same criteria the Neltje Blanchan Award, except that the recipient must be a woman. This award is also funded by Neltje.

Q. What type of artwork decorates the inside of the rotunda of the Wyoming State Capitol Building?
A. The rotunda is illuminated by panels of Tiffany-style stained glass.

Q. What are the ceilings of the Wyoming State Senate and House of Representatives chambers composed of?
A. The ceilings of both east and west wings of the Capitol building, where the House of Representatives and Senate are chambered respectively, are also composed of Tiffany-style stained glass, each ceiling including the Wyoming State Seal.

Q. What replica of a famous symbol of freedom from the American Revolutionary War adorns a corner of the Capitol Building property in Cheyenne? (Hint: The original is one of the most cherished Revolutionary War artifacts for Philadelphia, Pennsylvania.)
A. A replica of the Liberty Bell is on public display on the grounds of the Capitol Building. While other states also have replicas of the Liberty Bell, few others display it outside for anyone to view in passing.

Q. Four murals adorn the walls of both the House of Representatives chambers and the Senate chambers. The murals depict prominent characters from Wyoming history. Who painted them?
A. The Denver, Colorado artist Allen True painted them in 1917.

Q. How much was Allen True paid for each mural?
A. He was paid $500 for each mural.

Q. What is $500 in 1917 dollars worth today?
A. $7,617.

Q. One of the most ornate rooms of the Capitol Building is Legislative Conference Room 302. What illuminates this room?
A. A 1,000-pound Tiffany chandelier hangs from the ceiling to light this room.

Q. A large oil painting hangs in Legislative Conference Room 302 of the Wyoming State Capitol Building, entitled *Wyoming, the Land of the People, Past and Present*. What Powell, Wyoming native painted it?
A. Mike Kopriva created the painting. He is a professor of Fine Art at Northwest College in Powell, Wyoming.

Q. What other professor of fine art from Northwest College in Powell has a painting hung in the Wyoming State Capitol Building?
A. John Giarrizzo has a large painting, entitled *Here in this rocky passage*, in the rotunda of the Capitol Building.

SPORTS AND LEISURE

Q. What modern sport did Buffalo Bill's Wild West show and other traveling shows like it give birth to?
A. Cody's and other Wild West shows gave birth to modern rodeo. Ultimately, the shows became too expensive to produce, but the rodeos remained as a fixed event in local communities.

Q. Why do rodeo contestants call rodeos "shows" instead of competitions?
A. The rodeos are referred to as "shows" because they originated as segments of Wild West shows. A competitor refers to his or her efforts in any rodeo event as the "performance."

Q. Why is a belt buckle the standard award for a winning performance, instead of a tall trophy?
A. Many early professional rodeo competitors were often boxers as well. The standard award for a title in boxing is a buckle.

Q. What was the original name of the Professional Rodeo Cowboys Association?
A. The original name was the Cowboy Turtles Association.

Q. Why did the early professional cowboys name their organization "the turtles"?
A. In 1936, a group of sixty professional cowboys refused to compete in the Boston Garden Rodeo because the promoter reneged on paying prize money. The cowboy strike was effective. The cowboys decided to call their new bargaining organization The Cowboy Turtles Organization because they were slow to react to offense, but they would finally stick their necks out.

Q. What Wyoming city is designated the Rodeo Capital of the World?
A. Cody, Wyoming is designated the Rodeo Capital of the World. The Cody Night Rodeo is held every night of the week during the summer months. Cody was home base for its namesake, Buffalo Bill Cody, and the sport of rodeo had its beginnings in Wild West shows like William Cody's.

Q. Where was the first official rodeo held in Wyoming?
A. The first official rodeo was organized in Dayton, Wyoming in the 1880s. The contestants received no prize money, only the honor of winning.

Q. Where is the oldest rodeo held in Wyoming that first paid its contestants prize money?
A. Lander, Wyoming held the first "paid" rodeo in Wyoming and perhaps in the world.

Q. When was this rodeo held?
A. The first "paid" rodeo occurred on July 4, 1894 at the first Lander Pioneer Days.

Q. What is the nickname for the Pioneer Days Rodeo at Lander?
A. It is known as the "Granddaddy of 'Em All."

Q. Which Wyoming rodeo is known as the "Daddy of 'Em All?"
A. The Cheyenne Frontier Days Rodeo is known as the "Daddy of 'Em All."

Q. When was this rodeo first held?
A. Cheyenne's first Frontier Days occurred in 1897.

Q. What event in Greeley, Colorado was the Cheyenne Frontier Days designed to compete with, for tourist dollars?
A. The Frontier Days was held to draw tourists away from the Greeley Potato Days.

Q. Does a Potato Day still take place?
A. Yes, a small festival still takes place in Greeley, Colorado on September 9th to celebrate the potato harvest.

Q. What national business came up with the idea of Frontier Days and presented it to Cheyenne's fledgling Chamber of Commerce?
A. The Union Pacific Railroad created the concept of Frontier Days in hopes of increasing tourism to the Wyoming area.

Q. What is the largest rodeo in the world?
A. The Cheyenne Frontier Days Rodeo, which lasts ten days, is considered by many competitors to be the greatest rodeo to win, and is the largest outdoor rodeo in the world.

Q. How much does the population of Cheyenne, Wyoming increase by during Frontier Days?
A. Cheyenne will have over 600,000 visitors during Frontier Days, which will multiply its population by about sixfold.

Q. How much will a pancake breakfast cost a visitor to the Frontier Days?
A. Nothing; a free pancake breakfast has been one of the Frontier Days traditions in Cheyenne.

Q. How is the pancake batter mixed for so many people?
A. Cement trucks are used to stir the pancake batter.

Q. How many pancakes are usually served?
A. Over 100,000 pancakes are fried and served by the local Kiwanis club.

Q. What Wyoming cowboy holds the record for the most consecutive world Bareback Bronc Riding Titles?
A. Joe Alexander from Cora, Wyoming holds the record with five consecutive titles from 1971 to 1975. This also ties him with Bruce Ford for the record total number of Bareback Bronc titles ever won.

Q. What did Joe Alexander do astride a bronc named Marlboro at the Cheyenne Frontier Days in 1974?
A. He scored a 93 in bareback bronc riding competition, which was one of the highest recorded scores ever given in that competition in a Professional Rodeo Cowboy Association event. This score has been equaled several times, but surpassed only twice.

Q. What country and western singer and former rodeo star held the Bareback Bronc Riding title in 1976?
A. Chris LeDoux of Kaycee, Wyoming held the title in 1976.

Q. What foot does a Saddle Bronc Riding competitor always put in the stirrup first for good luck?
A. He puts his right foot in the stirrup first.

Q. What color is considered bad luck to be worn in rodeo competition?
A. Yellow is a bad luck color for a cowboy or cowgirl.

Q. What unusual fashion practice do rodeo cowgirls often utilize to bring good luck?
A. They wear mismatched socks.

Q. What bad luck may be brought on when a rodeo competitor throws their hat down upon a hotel room bed during a rodeo?
A. The bad omen may bring on an injury or even death to the cowboy or cowgirl.

Q. What is left out of pockets during rodeo competition?
A. Carrying loose change is considered bad luck because it may bring on small purse winnings or none at all.

Q. How long was the horse race that began in Evanston, Wyoming on May 30, 1908?
A. The race was seven days long, and traversed over 600 miles of wilderness, ending in Denver, Colorado.

Q. Were the famous endurance horse Hidalgo and his rider Frank Hopkins in this race?
A. No, Hidalgo never existed. The horse and his exploits was a myth, perpetrated by Hopkins to promote himself.

Q. What was the prize money for winning the race?
A. The winner received $2,500.

Q. Who sponsored the race?
A. The *Denver Post* sponsored the race.

Q. Was a movie ever made about the race?
A. Yes; released in 1975, it was called *Bite the Bullet*.

Q. Who starred in the movie?
A. Gene Hackman, Candice Bergen, James Coburn, Jan-Michael Vincent, and Ben Johnson starred in *Bite the Bullet*.

Q. There is a life-size statue of Sir Barton in Washington Park in Douglas, Wyoming. What is he famous for?
A. In 1919, he became the first thoroughbred horse to win the Triple Crown.

Q. What races must a horse win to have won the Triple Crown?
A. The horse must win the Kentucky Derby, the Preakness, and the Belmont Stakes.

Q. Why is his statue in a park in Douglas, Wyoming?
A. Sir Barton was pastured his last few years on a ranch near Douglas.

Q. Was Sir Barton born or trained in Wyoming?
A. No, he was sired and trained in Kentucky.

Q. How did Sir Barton wind up in Wyoming?
A. After being retired to stud, Sir Barton was sold to the U.S. Army Remount Service and stationed in Fort Robinson, Nebraska. He was sold by the army to a Douglas, Wyoming rancher.

Q. Sir Barton won the Triple Crown as a three-year-old horse. How many races of the six that he entered as a two-year-old did he win?
A. Sir Barton did not win any of the six.

Q. Was he expected to do well in the Kentucky Derby with more maturity as a three-year-old?
A. No, he was entered as a "rabbit" or a horse to take off at a high speed at the beginning off the race and tire all of the contenders so a stable mate could win. Sir Barton led the entire race and won by five lengths.

Q. Did Sir Barton win any other races in 1919 other than the three races of the Triple Crown?
A. Sir Barton actually won four races in a row. He raced at the Withers Stakes between the Preakness and the Belmont and won it as well, something no breeder or trainer has chanced since.

Q. How many races did Sir Barton win in 1919?
A. Sir Barton entered thirteen races of which he won eight, placed second in three, and third in two.

Q. What famous horse competed against Sir Barton and eclipsed his fame?
A. Man o' War, perhaps the most famous race horse of all time, began his career as Sir Barton began to fade as a four-year-old. Sir Barton was plagued with bad feet and an uncertain temperament, whereas Man o' War was a winner until he was retired to stud.

Q. What were Sir Barton's total career winnings?
A. His total winnings for three years of racing were $116,852.

Q. How much would $116,852 be worth in today's dollars?
A. $16.5 million.

Q. What does third place pay at the Kentucky Derby?
A. Third place pays $200,000, nearly twice what Sir Barton made in his entire career. Fourth place pays $100,000.

Q. What is the entrance fee for the Kentucky Derby?
A. The minimum cost is $50,600, but a breeder could pay in excess of $150,000.

Q. How much does the winner of the Kentucky Derby receive today?
A. The basic purse is $1,240,000, plus reimbursement of all entry fees. The Preakness and the Belmont pay about $600,000 apiece. There is a $5,000,000 bonus to any horse that wins the Triple Crown. (This does not even begin to include endorsements and future stud fees.)

Q. Where is the largest sled dog race in the Lower 48 states held?
A. The International Pedigree Stage Stop Sled Dog Race is held every year in the Rocky Mountains of western Wyoming.

Q. How many miles does the race cover?
A. The IPSSSDR covers nearly 450 miles in a loop through thirteen Wyoming towns.

Q. Where does the IPSSSDR begin?
A. The IPSSSDR begins and ends in Jackson Hole, Wyoming.

Q. Why is this race called a "stage stop" race?
A. The "stage stop" format refers to the fact that the race ends every night at a different Wyoming community. Mushers do not run their dogs indefinitely night and day as they do in the Alaskan Iditarod.

Q. Do dog mushers who compete in the Iditarod also compete in the IPSSSDR?
A. Yes. Susan Butcher (four time winner of the Iditarod), Jeff King (three time winner of the Iditarod), Rick Swenson (five time winner of the Iditarod), Bruce Lee (1998 winner of the Yukon Quest—considered to be the toughest sled dog race in the world), and Hans Gatt (three-time Yukon Quest winner), have all competed in the IPSSSDR.

Q. Did a man or a woman win the IPSSSDR in 2005?
A. A woman, Melanie Shirilla, won in 2005.

Q. What is the total purse for the IPSSSDR?
A. $100,000 is the total purse.

Q. What event challenges distance runners near Sheridan, Wyoming in the early summer?
A. The Bighorn Mountain Wild and Scenic Trail Run is a distance race held over mountain trails in the Bighorn Mountains in mid-June.

Q. How far do the competitors run?
A. Four races are held simultaneously: a 100-mile race, a 50-mile race, a 50-kilometer race, and a 30-kilometer race.

Q. What is the elevation change in the Bighorn Mountain Wild and Scenic Trail Run?
A. The races begin at nearly 4,000 feet above sea level and climb to over 10,000 feet at various points in the courses.

Q. What is the fastest winning time for the 100-mile race?
A. Jeff Browning of Bend, Oregon won the race in 2006 with a time of 20 hours, 24 minutes, and 28 seconds.

Q. What kind of sporting event is the Laramie Enduro?
A. The Laramie Enduro is a long-distance mountain bike race of 111 kilometers, or 70 miles.

Q. Where is "hang gliding heaven" in Wyoming?
A. Sand Turn on U.S. Route 14 a few miles east of Dayton, Wyoming on the eastern ascent of the Bighorn Mountains, is the site of some of the best hang gliding in the world.

Q. If a spectator stops at Sand Turn to observe hang gliders take off the ridge, what might he or she be asked to do?
A. If more than one person is a licensed driver in the vehicle, one of the spectators may be asked to shuttle the hang glider pilot's vehicle down the mountain to the landing area.

Q. What water sport benefits from the frequent winds of Wyoming?
A. Windsurfing is a very popular sport on many of the larger lakes of Wyoming.

Q. Where can one watch a polo match at the oldest polo club west of the Mississippi?
A. A person may watch a polo match any Sunday during the summer at the Big Horn Polo Grounds near Sheridan, Wyoming, established in 1898. It is one of the oldest polo clubs in the United States.

Q. Where have some of the finest polo ponies in the world been produced?

A. Many of the finest polo ponies in the world have come from the area around Sheridan, Wyoming.

Q. Frank Grouard was an umpire at one of the first organized polo tournaments in the Big Horn area. What was his nationality?
A. He was Polynesian.

Q. How did a Polynesian become an umpire at a polo match in Wild West Wyoming?
A. Grouard's father was a Mormon missionary to the South Pacific. The senior Grouard married a Polynesian woman and brought his family back to California.

Q. What famous person, whose face is carved upon a Black Hills mountain, was a friend of Frank Grouard?
A. Frank Grouard was captured by the Sioux Indians in 1870 and became the acquaintance of Crazy Horse, as well as Sitting Bull. Grouard had run away from his Mormon parents to live in Montana. He was under attack by Sioux warriors one day when Sitting Bull himself ordered the attack to stop because he was amused by the manner in which Grouard appeared in a bulky bearskin coat.

Q. What side did Frank Grouard participate on in the Indian Wars of the 1870s?
A. Frank Grouard became a scout for General Crook after he was liberated from the Sioux.

Q. What connection does Frank Grouard have with the Jim Gatchell Museum in Buffalo, Wyoming?
A. Frank Grouard became friends with a young Jim Gatchell and taught him the Sioux language. Gatchell consequently became friends with members of the Sioux tribe who gave him many artifacts. These became the core of the museum exhibits.

Q. What is Cowboy Polo?
A. Cowboy Polo is a variation of polo that is played once a year at the Big Horn Polo Grounds. Each team consists of three competitors, brooms are used instead of mallets, and a soccer ball is substituted for the regulation polo ball. Almost no rules apply, nor are there umpires to enforce them.

Q. What unique teams composed the annual Cowboy Polo match one year in the 1990s?
A. Cowboys took on a team of Crow Indians.

Q. What new regulation regarding the Indians' style of riding put them at an advantage in the match?
A. The Indians rode bareback and required the cowboy team to do the same. The cowboy players lost the game because they spent much of the match on the ground.

Q. Many couples have been married at the Big Horn Polo Club. What traditional celebration of anniversaries is sometimes practiced at the club?
A. Some couples wish to reminisce about their honeymoon, late at night in the center of the polo field on their anniversary.

Q. What old Roman sport has reappeared in Wyoming?
A. A form of horse-drawn chariot racing has become popular in Wyoming.

Q. Do the chariots have wheels?
A. Sometimes they do and sometimes they don't, depending on the season. Conventional chariots have wheels in the summer months or when no snow is available. Winter chariots or sleds with runners are sometimes referred to as cutters. Both types of chariots are pulled across the snow or mud track in a straight-line drag race.

Q. Is the driver strapped or fastened to the chariot in any manner?
A. No, fastening the driver to the chariot is against the rules.

Q. Is there a standard chariot design?
A. No, the only stipulation is that the weight of the driver, harness, and chariot combined must not exceed 275 pounds.

Q. What year did a hunter first need to purchase a license in the state of Wyoming?
A. 1899.

Q. How old is the One Shot Antelope Hunt competition of Lander, Wyoming?
A. It has been held every year since 1939.

Q. How is the competition won?
A. Three teams of eight members compete. Each team member is given one bullet. The team with the most antelope harvested in the least amount of time wins.

Q. What is benefited by the funds raised by the competition?
A. Water for Wildlife, which is a conservation organization that increases the number of watering holes for wildlife, benefits from the proceeds of the hunt.

Q. What valuable service do the Shoshone Indians provide for the hunters of the competition?
A. They perform the Blessing of the Bullets Ceremony to insure the steady aim of each hunter with his single bullet.

Q. Where was the largest Shiras moose trophy taken, according to the Boone and Crockett Club?
A. The world record Shiras moose was taken at Green River Lake, Wyoming in 1952 by John M. Oakley.

Q. What is a Shiras moose?
A. A Shiras moose is a subspecies of moose found in the Lower 48 states.

Q. What was the largest cutthroat trout caught in Wyoming?
A. A fifteen-pound, 32-inch rainbow trout was caught in 1959 by Alan Dow at Native Lake.

Q. What was the largest trout caught in Wyoming?
A. A lake trout caught in Flaming Gorge Lake by Andy Calkins in 1995 weighed fifty pounds and was 48 inches long. This is the largest fish caught in Wyoming on record.

Q. What rare animal can be legally trapped for domestication in Wyoming?
A. Falcons, both the peregrine and prairie varieties, may be trapped on a limited basis for use in falconry in Wyoming.

Q. May a person simply buy a falcon and then go out and hunt with the raptor?
A. No, a prospective falconer must train for two years under an established falconer to become licensed for owning his or her birds.

Q. Are falconers allowed to hunt in Wyoming?
A. Yes, they may hunt various species of game birds, including sage grouse, blue grouse, sharp-tailed grouse, and pheasant.

Q. How does a falconer prevent his falcon from simply flying away?
A. The falcon can actually fly away at any time during the hunting excursion. The bird has been conditioned from an early age to be familiar with humans and it relies upon its trainer/owner for food.

Q. How is the bird guaranteed to hunt?
A. The falconer carefully monitors the weight of his bird and regulates the amount of food that the falcon eats. If the falcon is hungry, it will hunt.

Q. Why do falconers save the molted or cast off feathers of their hunting birds?
A. Sometimes falcons lose or damage feathers in the process of hunting. The falconer can splice an old feather onto the stub of the damaged one so that the bird may still have optimum flight until a new feather grows in.

Q. What famous sportscaster was born and raised in Wyoming?
A. Curt Gowdy was born and raised in Green River, Wyoming in the 1920s and '30s.

Q. What did Wyoming bestow upon Curt Gowdy that he considered his greatest honor?
A. Curt Gowdy State Park, west of Cheyenne, was named in honor of him.

Q. What major league team did Curt Gowdy first announce games for?

A. He began announcing his first major league games for the New York Yankees.

Q. Where did Curt Gowdy go to announce major league games in 1951?
A. He went to announce for the Boston Red Sox, following Babe Ruth's career in reverse. The move did not help the Red Sox to win a pennant, as the Babe had helped the Yankees to accomplish several times.

Q. What was the name of the ABC network television program about hunting and fishing that Curt Gowdy hosted for many years? The show was one of his favorite projects.
A. "The American Sportsman" was the name of his favorite television project.

Q. What Casper, Wyoming-born major league baseball pitcher hurled a perfect no-hitter while playing for the Cincinnati Reds on September 16, 1988?
A. Left-hander Tom Browning.

Q. Did Tom Browning ever participate on a team that won the World Series?
A. Yes, the Cincinnati Reds won the World Series in 1990 with Tom Browning as an active pitcher on the roster.

Q. What practical joke cost Tom Browning a $500 fine from the team manager in 1993?
A. Tom Browning sneaked out of the dugout and entirely out of the stadium during a Reds versus Chicago Cubs game, when he was supposed to be available for immediate play. He appeared on a nearby rooftop, in uniform, for television cameras, apparently unmissed by the manager, Davey Johnson.

Q. Where can a person find more details about Tom Browning's career with the Cincinnati Reds?
A. Tom Browning has co-authored a book with Dann Stupp, entitled *Tom Browning's Tales From the Reds Dugout*.

Q. What other major league pitcher was born in Lusk, Wyoming?
A. Dick Ellsworth played in the major league from 1958 to 1971 for five different teams, most notably the Chicago Cubs.

Q. What Casper, Wyoming-born major league baseball outfielder played for five different teams in twelve years and hit 105 home runs?
A. Mike Devereaux.

Q. What Rawlins, Wyoming-born infielder played for three different major league teams?
A. Mike Lansing.

Q. What Kemmerer, Wyoming-born catcher currently plays for the Kansas City Royals?
A. John Buck.

Q. What Rock Springs, Wyoming-born athlete is currently playing for the Washington Redskins as a safety?
A. Adam Archuleta.

Q. What Evanston, Wyoming-born athlete is currently playing for the Green Bay Packers in the National Football League?
A. Brady Poppings.

Q. What Sheridan, Wyoming native won the first Professional Golf Association Tournament of America (PGA) that he entered as a pro?
A. Jim Benepe.

Q. What other PGA tournaments has Jim Benepe won?
A. None; the 1988 Beatrice Open in Oak Brook, Illinois was his only victory as a professional golfer in the PGA, although he had won other tournaments in other professional gulf leagues.

Q. What Afton, Wyoming native won a Gold Medal in the 2000 Olympics in the heavyweight division of Greco-Roman Wrestling?
A. Rulon Gardner.

Q. Who did Rulon Gardner defeat in the final match for the Gold Medal?
A. He defeated the Russian wrestler Alexander "The Experiment" Karelin for the medal.

Q. Why was Alexander Karelin nicknamed "The Experiment"?
A. Alexander was so successful as a wrestler that fans attributed his strength to the effects of some unknown Russian experiment.

Q. How many Gold Medals had Alexander Karelin won?
A. He had won Gold Medals in the previous three Olympics. He had been undefeated since 1987. No opponent had scored a single point against him in the six years before his match with Rulon Gardner.

Q. Did Rulon Gardner win any other Olympic medals?
A. Yes, he won a Bronze Medal in the 2004 Summer Olympics, in spite of having lost some toes in a snowmobiling accident.

Q. Who won the Silver Medal for the hammer throw in the 1996 Olympics in Atlanta, Georgia?
A. Lance Deal won a Silver Medal in 1996. He was born in Riverton, Wyoming.

Q. What Lander, Wyoming-based institution has been used by the United States Naval Academy, the National Park Service, and NASA to train some of their personnel?
A. The National Outdoor Leadership School in Lander, Wyoming has been used by all three organizations, as well as many other prominent organizations and companies.

Q. What is the purpose or mission of the National Outdoor Leadership School?
A. People attending NOLS learn environmental ethics, technical outdoor skills, and leadership skills for backcountry expeditions.

Q. Paul Petzoldt, the founder of the National Outdoor Leadership School, was a world-famous mountaineer. How old was he when he first climbed Grand Teton in Jackson Hole, Wyoming in 1924?
A. He was sixteen years old.

Q. Who was the youngest mountaineer ever to have climbed one of the peaks of the Grand Tetons?
A. Frank McClintock was the first mountaineer to climb the peak that would later bear his name. He climbed McClintock Peak at the age of ten, with his father, in 1901. The mountain is 11,005 feet tall.

Q. What is the motto of the Leave No Trace program begun by the NOLS?
A. "Take only photographs; leave only footprints" is the motto of the Leave No Trace program in respect to hiking in wilderness areas.

Q. Who is the youngest person to have climbed the Seven Summits, or the seven highest points of the seven continents of the Earth?
A. Britton Keeshan, who is a graduate of NOLS.

Q. Who was Britton Keeshan's famous grandfather?
A. Bob Keeshan, better known as Captain Kangaroo, was Britton Keeshan's grandfather.

Q. Britton Keeshan was very fond of his grandfather Bob. What did Britton do to honor the memory of his grandfather when he reached the summit of Mount Everest?
A. Britton buried a photograph of his grandfather and himself at the summit.

Q. What did Tori Murden McClure, another NOLS alumnus, accomplish in polar exploration?
A. In 1999, she was the first woman to ski to the South Pole.

Q. What amazing feat did Tori Murden McClure accomplish a little more than a year later?
A. She became the first woman and the first American to row across the Atlantic Ocean.

Q. What milestone has Christine Boskoff, another graduate of NOLS, reached in the sport of mountain climbing?
A. Christine Boskoff has climbed more 8,000-meter-high mountains (mountains in excess of 26,247 feet) than any other woman.

Q. Where was the first high school football game played under electric field lighting?
A. The first high school football game played under the lights was at Midwest, Wyoming in 1925.

Q. Where are the world's largest mineral hot springs located?
A. The hot springs of Thermopolis, Wyoming are the largest in the world.

Q. How many gallons per day are produced by the springs?
A. 18,600,000 gallons of water flow out of the springs in a 24-hour period. This would fill three Olympic-sized swimming pools.

Q. What is the temperature of the water?
A. The water emerges at 135 degrees Fahrenheit.

Q. How long have the hot springs been used for their healing properties?
A. The Native American population had used the hot springs since time immemorial. The United States government bought the land from the Shoshone Indians in 1897 and donated the hot springs area to the state of Wyoming for use by all people.

Q. Who insisted that some of the hot springs area be set aside for free public access?
A. Chief Washakie of the Shoshone tribe insisted upon some free public access as part of the land sale.

Q. Is use of the hot springs still free?
A. Yes, use of the hot spring water is still free at the state bath house. A small fee is charged for towels and bath house expenses.

Q. What state department was inadvertently created by the gift of the hot springs to Wyoming?
A. Hot Springs State Park became the first Wyoming State Park, thus creating the Wyoming State Parks Department.

Q. Are other places available to use the hot springs?
A. Yes. There are at least three other privately-owned spas in Thermopolis, where access to the hot springs water is available for a fee.

Q. Hot springs also once flowed near Casper, Wyoming at the town of Alcova.In the early 1900s, eastern development companies researched the possibility of developing a hot springs spa in this area, but decided to drop the project. Why?
A. The researchers decided that most Wyoming natives took a bath only on Saturday night.

Q. What Wyoming building did *Ripley's Believe It or Not* designate as the House of 69 Gables?
A. The Sheridan Inn in Sheridan, Wyoming qualified for this nickname.

Q. What famous Wyoming westerner helped build the Sheridan Inn and leased the first floor for his endeavors when it opened in 1893?
A. Buffalo Bill Cody had a large amount of input into the creation of the Sheridan Inn and leased its first floor as his base of operations. He owned a portion of the business for a few years. He auditioned performers for his Wild West show on the front porch. He later moved his center of operations to the hotel that he built in his namesake town, Cody, Wyoming.

Q. What famous author created some of his best work while staying at the Sheridan Inn?
A. Earnest Hemingway wrote some of his novel *A Farewell to Arms* while residing at the Sheridan Inn.

Q. Which U.S. President stayed at the Sheridan Inn?
A. Herbert Hoover stayed at the Sheridan Inn. in 1932, when he campaigned for reelection throughout the West.

Q. What famous actor, known for his years of USO entertainment of American troops, stayed at the Sheridan Inn?
A. Bob Hope stayed at the Sheridan Inn.

Q. What rope-spinning humorous cowboy from the depression era also stayed at the Sheridan Inn?
A. Will Rogers stayed at the Sheridan Inn.

Q. How much was the rate for one night's stay at the Sheridan Inn in 1893?
A. Customers paid one dollar a night.

Q. What is the current rate for a room at the Sheridan Inn?
A. The upper floors of the Sheridan Inn are currently undergoing renovation and are not available for occupation. A restaurant occupies the ground floor.

Q. Where did the huge, ornate bar that graces the Sheridan Inn come from?
A. The bar was constructed in England and shipped to Sheridan in the 1890s.

Q. What noise would remind a renter to turn the lights out at midnight at the Inn in 1893?
A. A steam whistle blew. The steam came from the coal-fired boiler that drove the steam engine that powered the generator providing electricity for the Inn.

Q. Where are the ashes of long-term Sheridan Inn employee Catherine Arnold, known as Miss Kate, interred?
A. Her ashes were interred inside a third floor wall within the room that she had occupied at the hotel during her 64 years of employment there. Miss Kate's friendly ghost is said to haunt the Inn.

Q. What major change was scheduled for the Sheridan Inn in 1965?
A. It was purchased by a developer and scheduled to be razed to make way for construction of a more modern building.

Q. Why wasn't the Sheridan Inn destroyed?
A. Local historical societies fought the destruction until Neltje Kings, a recent arrival to the area, purchased the property and renovated the ground floor. She operated a restaurant for several years. A restaurant still occupies the ground floor, but Neltje no longer owns the establishment.

Q. The Sheridan Inn is listed on the National Register of Historic Places, but it is in need of restoration throughout much of its structure. For a $1500 donation, where may a person have his or her name inscribed upon a brass plate in the hotel?
A. A donor's name will be placed upon a window sill in one of the sixty-nine gables of the Sheridan Inn.

Q. What will a $300 donation land a donor?
A. Three hundred dollars grabs the donor one brick-sized piece of the front sidewalk with his or her name on it.

Q. In what other building in Wyoming can a person walk in the footsteps of Buffalo Bill Cody for certain, as well as those of many other notable people?
A. William Cody built and frequented the Irma Hotel in Cody, Wyoming. He named it after his daughter.

Q. How close can a visitor get to the actual experience of turn-of-the-20th-Century Wyoming at the Irma Hotel?
A. A guest can rent a room in the old section of the Irma and sleep in the same period rooms that Buffalo Bill and many other famous people stayed in.

Q. Who gave the huge cherrywood bar to Buffalo Bill Cody, which now forms the centerpiece of the dining area of the Irma Hotel?
A. Queen Victoria of England gave the bar to Bill Cody. It was constructed in England.

Q. Where was the first brewery in Wyoming located?
A. The first brewery in Wyoming was located in the gold-mining town of Atlantic City.

Q. When was this brewery begun?
A. The brewery opened in 1868.

Q. Does the brewery still exist?
A. No, Atlantic City is a ghost town.

Q. What is horn hunting?
A. Horn hunting is the activity of hiking the wilderness areas of Wyoming, particularly in the early spring, to find and collect the dropped antlers of deer, elk, and the occasional moose.

Q. Of what use are these shed antlers?
A. Many people simply collect the antlers for their own enjoyment, but the antlers can be sold for decorative furniture or chandeliers. The antler is also sold for use in Asia, where its powder is believed to increase virility.

Q. What is the value of one pound of antlers?
A. The value of antlers varies, depending upon species of origin and condition. An average overall price would be $8.00 to $10.00 a pound. Bigger, matched sets can bring a lot more.

Q. What is the eighteen-foot-high arch that spans the Main Street of Afton, Wyoming composed of?
A. The arch is composed of interlocked elk antlers and is the largest of its kind in the world.

Q. When was this arch constructed?
A. The arch was built in 1958.

Q. How many antlers make up the arch?
A. Over 3,000 antlers compose the arch.

Q. Where is one of the world's finest and most popular aerobatic airplanes built?
A. The Pitts Special aerobatic biplane, used widely in stunt flying competition, is built in Afton, Wyoming.

Q. Where in Wyoming can a person rise 4,100 feet into the air without boarding an airplane or aircraft of any kind?
A. A person can ride the aerial tramway to the summit of Rendezvous Mountain in Jackson Hole. The peak is nearly 11,000 feet high. The tram carries 63 passengers at a time.

ENTERTAINMENT

Q. Where was country music performer and log-time resident of Kaycee, Wyoming, Chris Ledoux born?
A. He was born in Biloxi, Mississippi and raised in Tyler, Texas.

Q. What gives Chris Ledoux's songs about rodeo life authenticity?
A. He was a national bronc riding champion.

Q. In what Wyoming city did the progressive soul musical artist, Prince, choose to debut his movie *Under the Cherry Moon*?
A. Sheridan, Wyoming.

Q. Why did Prince choose Sheridan?
A. He did not actually choose Sheridan. MTV ran a contest in which Prince promised to release the movie in the hometown of the winner. Lisa Barber was the ten thousandth caller to dial the MTV hotline on the contest date and won a date with Prince to the premiere of his movie in Sheridan.

Q. After visiting Sheridan, Prince was asked what he thought of the town. What was his one-word response?
A. Prince uttered the enigmatic word, "Purple."

Q. How many silent movies were filmed in Wyoming?
A. Twenty-six silent movies were filmed in Wyoming.

Q. What young man was influenced by Buffalo Bill Cody's Wild West show in 1898 and first dreamed of becoming a cowboy?
A. Tim McCoy saw the Wild West show when he was a boy in Saginaw, Michigan.

Q. What did the young Tim McCoy do about it?
A. He came to Wyoming when he turned eighteen and became a cowboy on the Double Diamond Ranch.

Q. Why didn't Tim McCoy remain a cowboy?
A. He joined the army to fight in World War I.

Q. What rank did he ultimately attain?
A. At the end of World War I, he had reached the rank of lieutenant colonel, but he was promoted to Adjutant General of Wyoming, which really ranked him as a brigadier general.

Q. Why didn't General McCoy remain in the Army?
A. Tim McCoy had spent a lot of his early years living with the Shoshone and Arapaho Indians on the Wind River Reservation. He was hired by the movie industry to deal with the Indian extras in the silent films of the 1920s. Eventually, he began acting in the western movies.

Q. Did Tim McCoy act only in silent movies?
A. No, although his greatest stardom was during this era.

Q. What movie, based on a Jules Verne classic, did Tim McCoy act in, in 1956? Hint: This movie is not a western, although it has a western sequence in it.
A. *Around the World in Eighty Days* is the movie.

Q. Name some other famous actors who starred in this movie.
A. Any of the following would be correct: David Niven, Shirley Maclaine, Marlene Dietrich, or Frank Sinatra.

Q. How many Oscars did this movie win?
A. *Around the World in Eighty Days* was nominated for eight Oscars. It won five.

Q. What unusual record does this movie hold?
A. This movie holds the record for the most animals used in a production.

Q. What was the last movie that Tim McCoy starred in?
A. His final movie was *Requiem for a Gunfighter* in 1965.

Q. What did Tim McCoy do after his final movie?
A. He retired to his dude ranch near Thermopolis, Wyoming.

Q. What was the name of his dude ranch?
A. The ranch was called the H. E. Ranch.

Q. What did the Indians name Tim McCoy?
A. They called him "Nee Hee Chaoot," which meant "High Eagle," thus H. E. Ranch.

Q. What famous actress, who starred with Humphrey Bogart in the 1941 classic *High Sierra*, was born in the little town of Shoshone, Wyoming?
A. Isabel Jewell was born and raised in Shoshone.

Q. What movie about the French revolution and based upon a Charles Dickens novel did Isabel Jewell also star in?
A. The movie was *A Tale of Two Cities*, released in 1935 by MGM Studios.

Q. What famous Civil War romance movie of 1939 did Isabel Jewell have a role in?
A. She held a part in *Gone with the Wind*.

Q. What distinguished honor does Isabel Jewell have in Hollywood?
A. She has a star on the Hollywood Walk of Fame.

Q. What actor, born in Casper, Wyoming, played roles in the television series *Alf* and *Too Close For Comfort*, as well as appearing on the game show *Hollywood Squares?*
A. Jim J. Bullock.

Q. What was the first movie with sound filmed in Wyoming?
A. *The Big Trail* was filmed in 1930.

Q. What star had his first leading role in that film?
A. John Wayne. According to Walt Farmer, it may have been the first time that Wayne ever rode a horse, as well.

Q. Was John Wayne originally cast as the lead role in *The Big Trail?*
A. No, the director, Raoul Walsh, was supposed to play the lead role, but he had lost an eye in the filming of another movie.

Q. Was John Wayne the second choice for the lead role in *The Big Trail*?
A. No again! Raoul Walsh hoped to use Gary Cooper or Tom Mix.

Q. Why didn't Fox Film Corporation use Gary Cooper or Tom Mix?
A. Fox Films had lost a lot of money in the stock market crash and could not afford to pay for a big-name star and still film on location in Wyoming. The famous director of Westerns, John Ford, suggested they take a look at an extra working on another picture—John Wayne.

Q. What was John Wayne's real name?
A. Marion Morrison. It was changed to "John Wayne" for the billing for *The Big Trail*.

Q. How much was John Wayne paid for *The Big Trail*?
A. He was paid the huge salary of $75.00 per week. Established leading-man actors often earned over $200.00 a week.

Q. What other famous actors starred in *The Big Trail*?
A. Ward Bond and Tyrone Power.

Q. What other languages was *The Big Trail* presented in?
A. It was dubbed into Spanish, Italian, German, and French.

Q. Where in Wyoming were parts of it filmed?
A. Parts were filmed on the Snake River and in Moran, Wyoming.

Q. What Wyoming town was actually created by the film set of *The Big Trail*?
A. Moran Junction remained a town after the film crew left the buildings created for the filming of the movie.

Q. Was *The Big Trail* a success?
A. No, it actually contributed to Fox Film Corporation's filing for bankruptcy. *The Big Trail* was shot on a larger type of film, which required movie theatres to invest in special equipment to show it. Few were willing to do that.

Q. What was the first color movie filmed in Wyoming?
A. *Son of Lassie*.

Q. What countries was the film set in?
A. Norway and England.

Q. When was the movie filmed?
A. It was filmed during World War II and released in 1945.

Q. Where was the movie filmed in Wyoming?
A. Teton National Park.

Q. What major actors starred in the film?
A. June Lockhart, Peter Lawford, and the great canine actor Laddie.

Q. In 1952, what picture did Kirk Douglas star in, in which the Snake River doubled as the Missouri River?
A. *The Big Sky*, written by Montana author A. B. Guthrie.

Q. What famous Western was filmed in Jackson Hole in 1953 starring Alan Ladd, Ben Johnson, and Jack Palance?
A. *Shane*.

Q. How many Oscars did *Shane* win?
A. Only one: Loyal Griggs won an Oscar for cinematography. *Shane* was nominated in four other categories.

Q. What movie released in 1963 and filmed in Wyoming was also the basis for the television series *The Waltons*?
A. *Spencer's Mountain*, written by Earl Hammer.

Q. Where was the setting for *Spencer's Mountain*?
A. Jackson Hole, Wyoming.

Q. Where was the setting for *The Waltons*?
A. Virginia.

Q. What actor starred as the lead in the movie?
A. Henry Fonda.

Q. Who was the female lead?
A. Maureen O'Hara.

Q. What movie released in 1969 and partially filmed in Wyoming was based on the life of the famous oil rig fire fighter, Red Adair?
A. *Hellfighters.*

Q. Who was the lead actor (no stranger to filming in Wyoming)?
A. John Wayne.

Q. What movie was released in 1977 in which a large part of the movie took place at Devils Tower, Wyoming?
A. *Close Encounters of the Third Kind.*

Q. Who directed *Close Encounters of the Third Kind*?
A. Steven Spielberg.

Q. What major actors portrayed characters in the film?
A. Richard Dreyfuss and Teri Garr.

Q. What is a close encounter of the third kind?
A. Actual face-to-face or physical contact with a being from an Unidentified Flying Object.

Q. What place in Wyoming was the setting for the movie *Cat Ballou,* starring Lee Marvin and Jane Fonda and released in 1965?
A. Wolf City, Wyoming.

Q. How many people live in Wolf City now?
A. Perhaps a dozen or so. Wolf City is more of a pleasant crossroads between two gravel roads near Sheridan, Wyoming. It has no post office and really only exists as a name on a map.

Q. What famous actor from *The Lord of the Rings* trilogy starred in a horror movie entitled *Prison* that was filmed in the Wyoming Territorial Prison in Rawlins?
A. Viggo Mortensen, who played Aragorn in *The Lord of the Rings*.

Q. How did Viggo Mortensen's character die in the movie, *Prison?*
A. He was executed in the electric chair Viggo Mortensen actually broke the arms on the prop electric chair in his violent portrayal and the chair had to be repaired.

Q. Does Wyoming have an electric chair?
A. No, the chair used for restraining prisoners during execution was removed from the gas chamber at the Wyoming State Prison and a movie prop electric chair was installed.

Q. What injury did extras suffer due to Wyoming's higher altitude?
A. While standing in their underwear to shoot one scene repeatedly, extras were sunburned in the thinner Wyoming air because they were not issued sunscreen.

Q. What famous horror movie actress autographed a poster from one of her movies to be displayed as decoration for a prison cell in the movie *Prison?*
A. Linda Blair, of *The Exorcist* fame, was visiting a friend on the set and autographed her poster.

Q. What movies did director Renney Harlin direct, other than *Prison?*
A. He directed *Diehard 2* and *Cliffhanger*.

Q. What picturesque place near Casper, Wyoming served as the movie set for the movie *Starship Troopers* in 1997?
A. The area known as Hell's Half Acre, a badlands area 40 miles west of Casper, Wyoming.

Q. Large alien bugs are seen in the movie *Starship Troopers*. Their images were created by a Phil Tippett. What other famous other-worldly creatures did Tippett create?
A. He created the dinosaurs for *Jurassic Park*.

Q. Why was movie staff member Rock Golotti nearly hauled off for a very long stay in the Wyoming prison system when he was stopped for speeding on his way to the set at Hell's Half Acre?
A. The back seat of the car that he was driving was covered with very lethal looking prop weapons for use in filming. Rock Golotti was the weapons master for the movie.

Q. What 2005 movie by author E. Annie Proulx brought attention to Wyoming?
A. *Brokeback Mountain* focused attention upon the lonely life of sheepherders in Wyoming and the conservative nature of Wyoming's small towns in the 1960s.

Q. Did *Brokeback Mountain* win any Academy Awards?
A. Yes, it won three. The movie won Best Director, Best Adapted Screenplay, and Best Musical Score.

Q. Is E. Annie Proulx a native of Wyoming?
A. No, she has been a resident of Wyoming since 1993. She is from New England.

Q. What brought E. Annie Proulx to Wyoming?
A. She spent several months in fellowships at the Ucross Foundation for the Arts retreat in Ucross, Wyoming.

Q. Mary O'Hara, a Wyoming author, wrote the popular children's book *My Friend Flicka*. How many movies have been made of the book?
A. Two. *My Friend Flicka* was made by Fox Studios in 1943 and *Flicka* was released by Fox Studios again in 2006.

Q. What famous country and western singer starred in the 2006 version of *Flicka*?
A. Tim McGraw starred in the 2006 movie, playing the part of the father of a child who wished to ride the wild horse Flicka.

Q. Was the child main character a boy or girl in the 2006 version of *Flicka*?
A. The child was a girl, portrayed by Alison Lohman.

Q. Was the child main character a boy or girl in the novel by Mary O'Hara?
A. The main character was a boy.

Q. Who played the child main character in the 1943 version entitled *My Friend Flicka*?
A. Roddy McDowell played the young boy who wanted to ride the wild horse Flicka in the 1943 version.

Q. Were there other Mary O'Hara stories adapted to movies?
A. Yes, at least two. *Thunderhead, Son of Flicka* was released as a sequel to *My Friend Flicka* in 1945. It was followed by *The Green Grass of Wyoming* in 1948.

Q. Was *My Friend Flicka* ever adapted to the small screen?
A. Yes, *My Friend Flicka* was a television series from 1956 to 1958.

Q. What Steven Spielberg movie is based upon the 1943 version of *My Friend Flicka*?
A. Steven Spielberg's extraterrestrial hit *ET* is based on *My Friend Flicka*.

Q. What Cheyenne, Wyoming-born actress was married to Charlie Chaplin at the age of sixteen?
A. Mildred Harris.

Q. How old was Charlie Chaplin at the time?
A. He was twenty-nine.

Q. This marriage lasted two years. What famous person did Mildred Harris have a romantic relationship with for a brief time after her divorce?
A. She was involved with the Prince of Wales who later became King Edward VIII of England.

Q. Edward VIII was forced to abdicate his crown in 1936. Why?
A. He had fallen in love with another American girl, Wallis Simpson—twice divorced and totally unacceptable for the British to accept as Queen.

Q. What series of silent movies did Mildred Harris star in that later made Judy Garland famous when remade as talkies?
A. Mildred Harris starred in two silent movies based on *The Wizard of Oz*, in 1914: *The Magic Cloak of Oz* and *His Majesty, the Scarecrow of Oz*.

Q. Mildred Harris was a favorite of what famous director?
A. Cecil B. DeMille.

Q. Mildred Harris acted in silent movies with such noted stars as Douglas Fairbanks, Sr., Tyrone Power, Clara Bow, and Lionel Barrymore. She also starred in a "talkie" with a famous comedy trio. Name that trio.
A. In 1936, she starred in *Movie Maniacs* with the Three Stooges.

Q. What recent Robert Redford movie was based on a book by Cody, Wyoming author Mark Spragg?
A. *An Unfinished Life*, released by Miramax Studios in 2005, was written by Mark Spragg.

Q. Where did Mark Spragg grow up?
A. He spent his childhood on his family's dude ranch located between Cody and Yellowstone National Park.

Q. What is the setting for *An Unfinished Life?*
A. The story takes place on a ranch in Wyoming.

Q. What actor who starred in *Unforgiven* and *The Shawshank Redemption* also starred in *An Unfinished Life?*
A. Morgan Freeman.

Q. What shapely pop music songstress also starred in *An Unfinished Life?*
A. Jennifer Lopez.

Q. What famous lasso-spinning humorist of the early 20th Century starred in the 1933 movie, *Mr. Skitch*, which was filmed in Wyoming?
A. Will Rogers starred in *Mr. Skitch*.

Q. In the 1939 movie *Down the Wyoming Trail*, also filmed in Wyoming, how did the rustlers hide the cattle that they had stolen?
A. The cattle were hidden in an elk herd.

Q. In the 1998 movie *Wind River*, what real-life Pony Express rider is befriended by Chief Washakie of the Shoshone Indian tribe?
A. Elijah "Nick" Wilson was a Mormon boy who rode on the Pony Express and was also adopted by the Shoshone Indians. Wilson recorded his life in an autobiography entitled *Nick Wilson, Pioneer Boy Among the Indians.*

Q. What Wyoming town is named for him?
A. Wilson, Wyoming, located in the northern part of Jackson Hole, is named for Nick Wilson.

Q. What theatrical event draws visitors back in history on the second Sunday of July every year in Pinedale, Wyoming?
A. The Sublette County Historical Society presents a reenactment of the mountain man rendezvous held near present-day Pinedale during the early years of the 19th Century. All costumes worn in the pageant are authentic in every detail.

Q. When were the original mountain man rendezvous held?
A. The gatherings of fur trappers, Indians, and mountain men occurred in the month of July between the years of 1825 and 1840.

Q. What was the purpose for the rendezvous?
A. Mountain men traded their furs for supplies for the coming year. A caravan brought the supplies overland from Saint Louis, Missouri.

Q. Why did the rendezvous end?
A. Fashion trends in Europe began to favor silk hats instead of beaver-felt hats, and an influx of people and the Oregon Trail into Wyoming rendered the supply caravans pointless.

Q. What strange gift was given to the famous mountain man Jim Bridger at the 1837 rendezvous?
A. Jim Bridger was reportedly given a suit of English medieval armor by his fellow mountain men as a joke. It is unknown where the armor came from or why it was given to Bridger.

Q. What Wyoming outdoor activities training institute did the actor Andrew McCarthy attend?
A. He graduated from the National Outdoor Leadership School in Lander, Wyoming.

Q. What famous director of mountain climbing movies graduated from the National Outdoor Leadership School?
A. David Breashears is a famous mountaineer and filmmaker who has worked on such well-known movies as *Cliffhanger* and *Seven Years in Tibet*. He graduated from NOLS.

Q. What actress of B movies from the 1940s, and known as the "Venezuelan Volcano," was born in Cheyenne, Wyoming?
A. Burnu Acquanetta.

Q. What was the name of the Tarzan series movie that she acted in?
A. *Tarzan and the Leopard Woman.*

Q. What famous children's comedy troupe, created by Hal Roach, did Richard "Mickey" Daniels belong to?
A. "Mickey" Daniels was part of the *Our Gang* or *Little Rascals* cast. He was born in Rock Springs, Wyoming.

Q. What Wyoming native appears on the television series *Lost* as Dr. Jack Shepard?
A. Matthew Fox plays the part of Dr. Jack Sheppard. He was born and raised on a horse ranch in Crowheart, Wyoming.

Q. What honor was bestowed upon Matthew Fox by *People* magazine in 1996?
A. He was voted one of the Fifty Most Beautiful People in the World.

Q. What 2006 movie about a football team killed in a plane crash does Matthew Fox star in, along with Matthew McConaughey?
A. *We Are Marshall* is a movie about the November 14, 1970 plane crash that killed 37 members of the Marshall University football team of West Virginia, and its effects on the survivors.

Q. Where in Wyoming can a visitor become the star of his or her own short movie?
A. Wyoming Innovations is a film production company based out of the Dayton Mercantile building in Dayton, Wyoming. A segment of this company, named Studio G, will produce a very short film of the client in front of a device called a "green screen." The new actor is coached through a predetermined script while he or she is in costume. The actor's performance is grafted into the pre-filmed movie by the magic of the green screen. The completed movie is ready for the client within a day or two. The cost of the personalized movie is about $65. Several scripts are available.

Q. What Cheyenne-born science fiction writer co-wrote the novel and classic science fiction movie *Logan's Run?*
A. George Clayton Johnson co-wrote *Logan's Run*. He also wrote several stories for *The Twilight Zone* and *Star Trek*.

Q. What famous Rat Pack movie was based upon one of George Clayton Johnson's short stories?
A. *Ocean's Eleven*.

Q. In what science-fiction television series does a spaceship named the *Wyoming* appear?
A. The *Wyoming* is a sister ship to the *Enterprise* in an episode of *Star Trek*.

Q. Is there a precedent for naming ships after the state of Wyoming in the United States Navy?
A. Yes, a submarine named *Wyoming* is currently in service with the U.S. Navy.

Q. Is this the only ship to have been named *Wyoming?*
A. No, three previous U.S. Navy ships have been named *Wyoming*, although the first of the three was named after the Wyoming Valley in Pennsylvania.

Q. What actor, born in Cheyenne, Wyoming, appeared in both *The Texas Chainsaw Massacre* and *The Texas Chainsaw Massacre II?*
A. Jim Siedow.

Q. What Cheyenne theatre group has been in existence for over 75 years?
A. The Cheyenne Little Theatre Players group has been in existence since 1930.

Q. The demise of what cultural staple of the 19th Century brought about the beginnings of the Cheyenne Little Theatre Players?
A. Professional theatre groups used to travel throughout the country giving presentations in towns of all sizes. Towns like Cheyenne depended upon these groups to bring a bit of culture and entertainment into the West. These traveling actors groups gradually disappeared in the beginning of the 20th Century, so

the elite of Cheyenne society sought to create their own theatre from within their own ranks.

Q. Is the Cheyenne Little Theatre Players group only open to Cheyenne's more affluent citizens?
A. Certainly not. The theatre group is open to all individuals. In its beginning, only members of higher society had the time and resources to participate.

Q. What is one of the mainstay productions of the Cheyenne Little Theatre Players during the summer months and prime tourist time?
A. The *Old Fashioned Melodrama* is a production of classic old-style western melodrama, often written by local talent, for people of all ages and tastes. One memorable title of the past was *She Was Chaste on the Plains and Won in the West*.

Q. What building, listed on the National Register of Historic Places, is used for the productions of the Cheyenne Little Theatre Players?
A. The Atlas Theatre building is the site of the *Old Fashioned Melodrama* and other Cheyenne Little Theatre Players productions. It is located at 213 West 16th Street in Cheyenne.

Q. What was the name of the night club that once occupied the Atlas Theatre?
A. The night club was named The Pink Pony.

Q. How many figure skating clubs are located in Wyoming?
A. Four figure skating organizations exist in Wyoming. They are centered at ice arenas in Rock Springs, Cody, Casper, and Jackson Hole.

Q. What Sheridan, Wyoming resident portrays Buffalo Bill Cody in educational and entertainment presentations for various organizations and gatherings?
A. William Frederick Boycott portrays Buffalo Bill Cody. He is a member of the New Christy Minstrels and is listed on the Wyoming Arts Council Roster of Artists.

Q. How many symphony orchestras exist in Wyoming?
A. Two symphony orchestras exist in Wyoming, the Wyoming Sym-

phony Orchestra, based in Casper, and the Cheyenne Symphony Orchestra.

Q. What Sheridan, Wyoming-based band is internationally known and has opened for such performers as Bob Dylan and Kid Rock?
A. The band is called Simply Jane.

Q. What Wyoming-based blues band traces its beginnings to the Pi-A-Rib Café in Laramie, Wyoming and has played with such famous blues musicians as Buddy Guy and Taj Mahal?
A. Blinddog Smokin'.

Q. What punk rock band from Newcastle, Wyoming has released CDs entitled *Death by Television* and *The Too Late Show?*
A. The Lillingtons.

Q. What Wyoming cowboy-turned musician was referred to by Meredith Ochs, a writer for *Rolling Stone*, as "a treasure trove of country blues"?
A. Michael Hurwitz.

Q. What accordion player from Rock Springs, Wyoming has been inducted into the Ironworld Discovery Center Polka Hall of Fame?
A. Richard Kaumo.

Q. In what Wyoming city has a jazz festival taken place every year since 1988?
A. The Yellowstone Jazz Festival has taken place in Cody, Wyoming annually since 1988.

Q. What well known Mexican fast food chain had its beginnings in Cheyenne, Wyoming?
A. The Taco John's fast food restaurant chain began in Cheyenne, Wyoming in 1968.

Q. Was Taco John's the name of the first restaurant in Cheyenne?
A. No, the first restaurant was named Taco House and was started by John Turner. He sold the business to Jim Woodsen and Harold Holmes. They renamed the restaurant Taco John's and slowly expanded the chain.

Q. How many Taco John's restaurants exist today?
A. Over 420 Taco John's in 24 states exist today.

Q. Which Wyoming bar received the first liquor license in the state after prohibition was lifted in 1937?
A. The Million Dollar Cowboy Bar in Jackson Hole received the first liquor license issued in 1937. The bar was owned by Ben Goe.

Q. Why is the bar called the Million Dollar Cowboy Bar?
A. The bar top is completely covered by silver dollars.

Q. What are some of the bar stools made of in the Million Dollar Cowboy Bar?
A. The bar stools are topped by actual saddles.

Q. The Million Dollar Cowboy Bar has furniture and wood work crafted by hand from local knobbled pine. Are there any other bars in Wyoming with this style of furniture and wood work?
A. The Mint Bar of Sheridan, Wyoming, for one example, also has this unusual style of décor.

Q. What do the framed photographs lining the walls of the Mint Bar depict?
A. The photographs are of contestants in the Sheridan rodeos over the past years.

Q. What is embedded in the shingled walls of the Mint Bar?
A. Ranch brands are stamped into the shingles.

Q. How big is the rattlesnake hide that hangs over the bar in the Mint Bar?
A. The hide is 8 feet 4 inches long and has 37 buttons on its rattle.

Q. What country music star was tossed through the plate glass window of the Mint Bar in the filming of the TV movie *Wild Horses* in 1985?
A. Kenny Rogers.

Q. How long has the Mint Bar been in business?
A. The Mint Bar has been open since 1907.

Q. What Cody, Wyoming bar has been a favorite stop for county music performers such as Vince Gill and Tanya Tucker?
A. Cassie's Supper Club and Dance Hall has witnessed impromptu performances by famous guests Vince Gill and Tanya Tucker, accompanied by Cassie's house band, West.

Q. Was Cassie's always a supper club and dance hall?
A. Yes and more. In its beginnings it was a house of "soiled doves." Cassie Waters was the madame and owner of the establishment at its beginning in 1933.

Q. A parrot is Cassie's official symbol. Why?
A. Olle and Mabel Nelson took over ownership of Cassie's in 1955. They had two parrots as pets and thus chose the parrot as their business symbol.

Q. The Woods Landing Dance Hall is listed on the National Register of Historic Places. What is unique about its construction?
A. The dance hall floor was constructed on top of twenty-four railroad boxcar springs to lessen the shock to dancers' legs and to ease the stress on the structure of the building.

Q. What strange object was found in a cave by prospectors in the Pedro Mountains of south-central Wyoming in 1932?
A. A tiny human mummy was found seated in a fetal position in the cave. People believed the mummy to be of some pygmy race or evidence of the "little people" of Crow Indian legend. These "little people" were somewhat like European leprechauns or fairies.

Q. What strange sight could prove dangerous to travelers near Morrissey, Wyoming?
A. Many years ago, strange, bright lights, called ghost lights, floated near the highway, causing drivers to veer off the road to avoid them and crash. The source of the lights has never been explained.

Q. What problems might visitors to the Ivy House Inn, located in Casper, Wyoming, have with their vehicles?
A. If an automobile is parked in a certain location in the parking lot, where the living room of a house used to be located, a ghost may set off the theft alarm. This usually happens after 2:30 a.m. or in late morning. The house that formerly occupied the parking lot area was haunted by a ghostly presence in the sitting room, which seems to have remained.

Q. Are there any other spirits at the Ivy House Inn Bed and Breakfast?
A. Yes, the ghost of a former female owner often travels from room to room, while the ghosts of her cats are seen running up and down the halls and stairway.

Q. Does any ghost haunt the Irma Hotel in Cody, Wyoming?
A. Yes, Irma herself, often referred to as the White Lady, often visits the hotel rooms upstairs. Also, a soldier from the time of the Indian wars is sometimes witnessed at the cherrywood bar.

Q. What action by an audience member may spell trouble for the performance on stage at the Natrona County High School in Casper?
A. If an audience member sits in a certain chair that is believed to be haunted by the ghost of a deceased student who loved to participate in the performing arts, problems or disasters will befall the production being witnessed. This particular chair seems to always remain folded down as if occupied at all times. The springs of the chair have been replaced—even the entire chair has been replaced—but the seat remains down.

Q. If a traveler passes the Wyoming State Hospital in Evanston, Wyoming and notices a sheet hung in a window to obscure the view within, what might the sheet be concealing?
A. A young woman hanged herself once at the hospital and her ghost might be seen repeating the suicide in the room. Lights may be turned on at night, even though power has been cut off to the room.

Q. Fort Bridger, Wyoming seems to be crawling with ghosts of every kind. What particular animal ghost has a kinship with Lassie?
A. The ghost of a dog that saved a boy and was decorated by the army for this act of heroism haunts the grounds of Fort Bridger.

Q. What is the Laramie Ghost that returns every seven years to Fort Laramie?
A. The Lady in Green, or the Laramie Ghost, is the spirit of a young woman who came to stay with her father at Fort Laramie in the mid-1800s. She went riding alone out on the plains against her father's wishes and was never seen again. Her ghost reportedly returns to the area every seven years and has been witnessed by many people. Army records officially document a sighting by a Lt. Alison in 1871.

ABOUT THE AUTHOR

Brian Day lives in a small town at the base of the Bighorn Mountains in north-central Wyoming with his wife Joelle, two cats, and two dogs. He makes his living in construction and hopes to further his writing career.

Q. *Are there other fun, interesting books about Wyoming?*
A. *Yes! Look for these books at your local bookstore or call Riverbend Publishing toll-free 1-866-787-2363*
www.riverbendpublishing.com

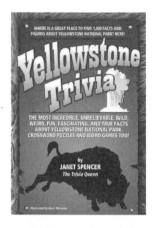

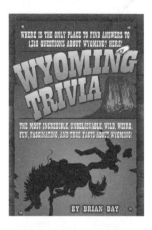

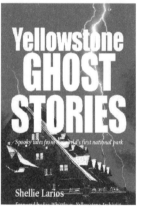

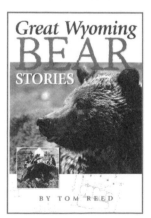

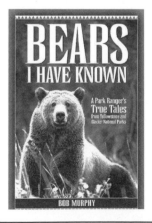